CHARLES-LOUIS HANON

THE VIRTUOSO PIANIST

New edition with
supplementary exercises by
Otto Weinreich

English translation by
Renate Maria Wendel

EIGENTUM DES VERLEGERS · ALLE RECHTE VORBEHALTEN
ALL RIGHTS RESERVED

EDITION PETERS

LONDON · FRANKFURT/M. · LEIPZIG · NEW YORK

PREFACE

A new edition of this popular technical study-book seems particularly useful as the approach to the mastery of such material has changed considerably. The former habit of endless repetition of the same exercise in order to "grind off" its inherent technical problems is practically outmoded nowadays. Instead one should endeavour to overcome faulty execution by singling out the individually varying problems and concentrating on these – often only one finger, a certain interval or a few phrases – in special exercises. This selective and special treatment of difficulties means efficient study, saves time, leads to quicker results, and, equally important, it enlivens the player's work. This method of practice, however, demands constant concentration and puts an end to a mechanical "casual" way of playing. Different accentuation alone requires special attention, and rhythmication leads to complex demands on the ear. Contrary motion, imitation and different articulation for each hand, transposition etc., are musically demanding enough to be suggestive no longer of dry technical exercises. Thus Hanon's "Virtuoso Pianist" will come alive.

It is the task of the teacher or the intelligent student to select what they require from the given variants: not every student – sometimes not even both hands of the same student – will need the same variant.

Detailed instructions for the technique of touch have generally not been included in order not to restrict the possibilities of execution. Anyway, it is the teacher's task to include these in the individual lesson.

One should aim to relate the exercises to their practical use. Sometimes fingering has been given for which the reason (apart from carrying out the instructions) will only become apparent in the context of more recent music, where it may simplify things.

Some instructions in the original edition have been retained on account of their "historical" value. On the whole, however, the order and sequence of the exercises remained unchanged.

OTTO WEINREICH

We quote the following passages from the original edition to illustrate the intentions of Hanon and his times:

"If the five fingers of each hand were developed equally, they would be able to perform everything written for this instrument, the only problem remaining being the fingering, which could be solved easily."

"This work can be played through in one hour from beginning to end, and once mastered completely and repeated daily for a while all problems will vanish as if by magic."

(Hanon)

© Copyright 1987 by Hinrichsen Edition
Peters Edition Limited, London

THE VIRTUOSO PIANIST
PART ONE

Preparatory exercises to acquire agility, independence, strength and perfectly even development of the fingers.

*

To practise the 20 finger-exercises in Part One start with the metronome set at 60 and gradually increase up to 108: hence the two metronome marks at the beginning of each exercise.

No. 1

Separate and lift the fingers well to make every note audible as distinctly as possible.

Important: Proceed chromatically through all major keys!

Variations to exercise No. 1

1.

2.

3. In sixths — or

4.

5. descending — Exchange rhythms of right and left hand when descending.

6. *pp* ... *mf* Practise also with hands crossed.

7. Similarly, practise the augmentation in the right hand, the variation in demisemiquavers in the left.

1st case or portamento
Contrary motion

8.

With exaggerated rotary movement in alternating hands!

9. Very fast

10.

Also with this rhythm!

and — and

Note: Whole tone scale (see p. 54)

11.

No. 2

For brevity from now on only the numbers of the fingers to be specially trained by each exercise will be indicated, e.g. 3rd and 4th finger for the second exercise, 2nd, 3rd and 4th finger for the third exercise.

No. 3

No. 4

No. 5

No. 6

No. 7

A delight for beautifully exaggerated finger movements (even though abhorrent to some!)

leggiero

and descending

Very fast

No. 8

1
2
3 Right hand alone and left hand alone
Also in 6/8 :
3a
3b
4
R.
L.
5 Hands separately for the whole exercise
8

No. 9

Extension of 4th and 5th finger and all-finger exercise

1

2 Practise also in triplets

3

4 Stretch!

No. 10

No. 11

or cut out every second bar and proceed directly to the next step

No. 12

No. 13

No. 14
Preparation for the trill using the 3rd and 4th fingers

17

18

13 Whole tone

Can also be played with hands crossed – one octave apart

No. 15

Also with the following fingerings: **2 3, 3 4, 4 5**.

10. Whole tones. – Also arpeggiated in semiquavers.

Ascend also chromatically through whole-tone scales – i.e. alternate between 1st bar of *a)* and 1st bar of *b)* etc.

No. 16

Extension of 3rd and 5th finger and exercise for the 3rd, 4th and 5th fingers.

No. 17

No. 18

Also accentuated in triplets

No. 19

Also play this exercise with either upper or lower part *staccato*

No. 20

PART TWO

No. 21

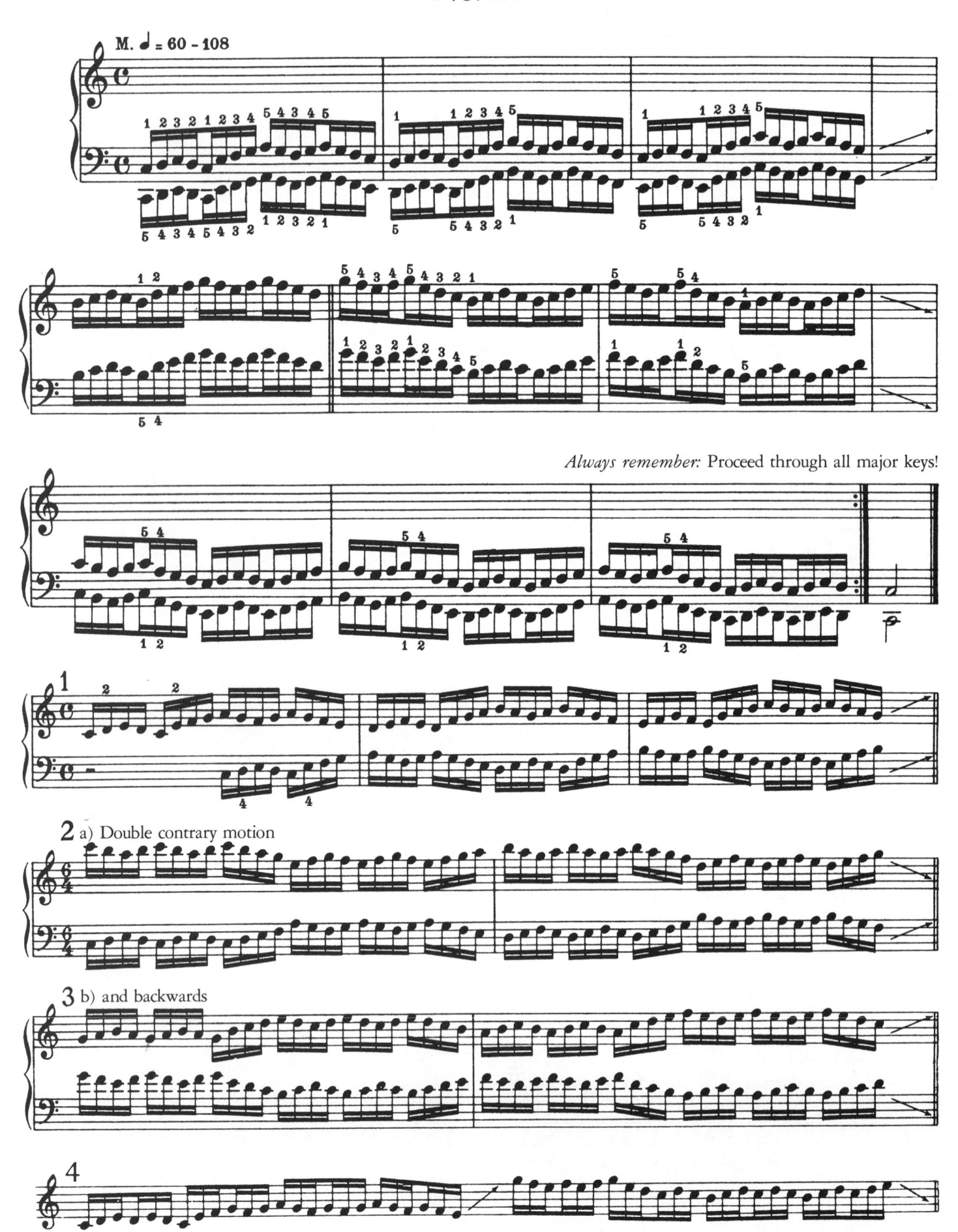

Always remember: Proceed through all major keys!

2 a) Double contrary motion

3 b) and backwards

No. 22

26

No. 23

2 Very quick – delayed octaves
3
4
5
6
Proceed diatonically
7
Proceed chromatically
8

No. 24

No. 25

No. 26

No. 27
Preparation of the 4th and 5th fingers for the trill shown further on.

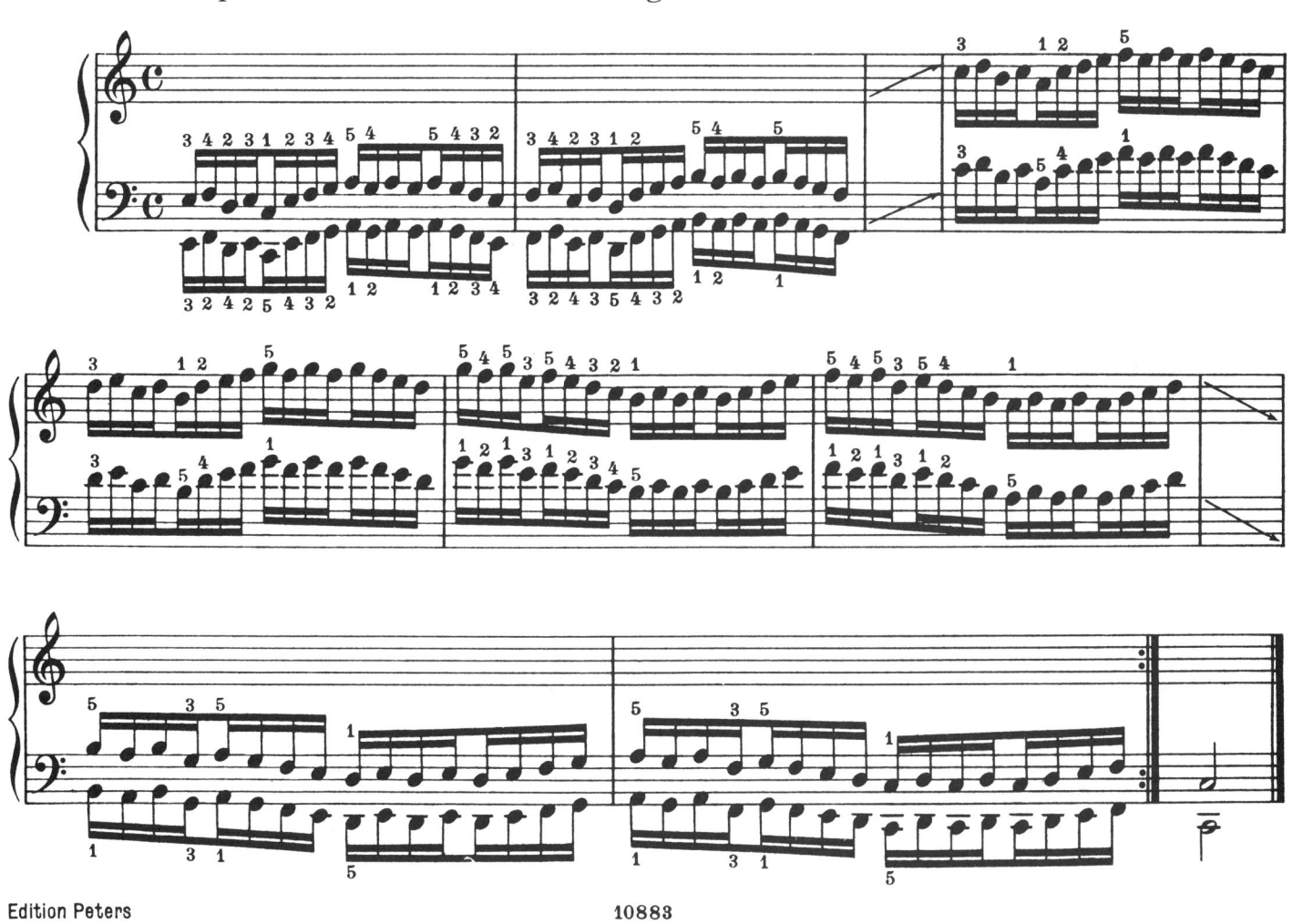

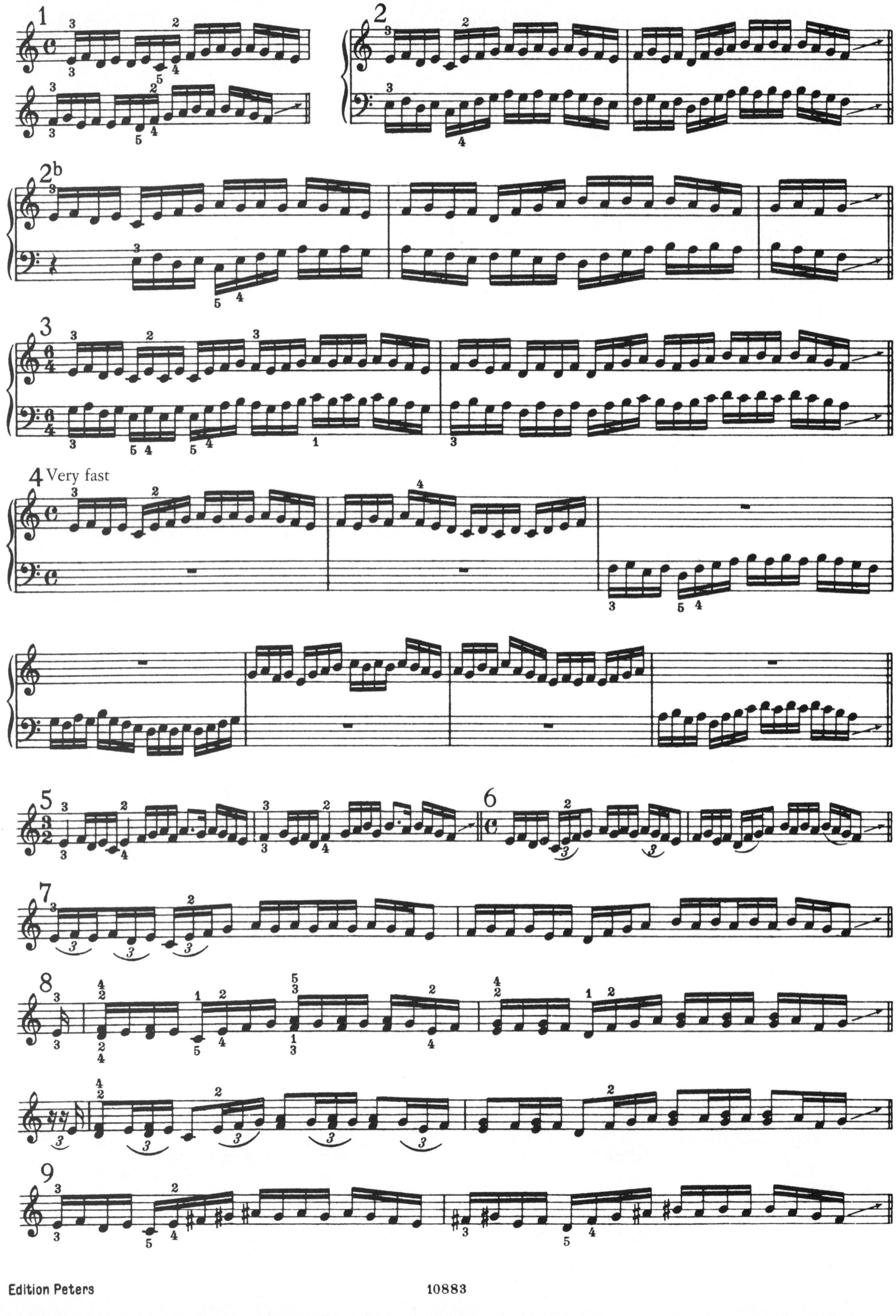
1
2
2b
3
4 Very fast
5
6
7
8
9

No. 28

No. 29
Preparation for the trill for all five fingers

9 or alternating

10 occasionally with the following fingering

No. 30

Trill, alternating between 1st and 2nd and 5th and 4th fingers.

No. 31

It is beneficial to do Exercise No. 37 before this and the following exercises.

No. 32
Passing under the thumb with the hand moving on

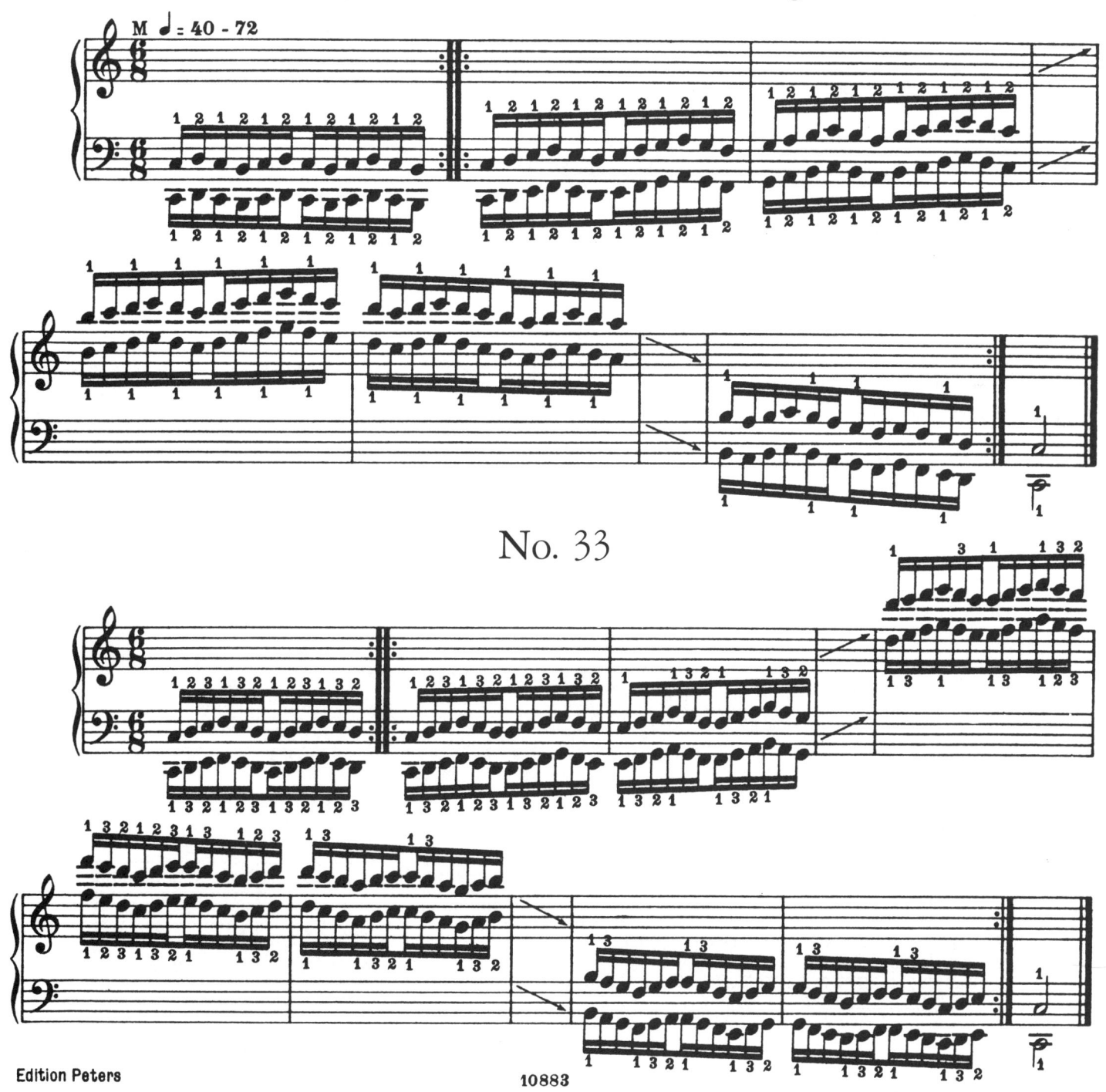

No. 33

No. 34

Also in contrary motion
Whole-tone
Ascending right
Descending left
Ascending right
Descending left

No. 35

No. 36

No. 37
Special exercise for passing under the thumb

The entire parallel movement is executed by the thumbs only.
Hold down the chord silently, or better still, just touch the keys without pressing them down.

1a Positions for passing under in the E major scale

1b Change of position in the E major scale

2 Right only — Left only

Always with swing

4b Passing under and stretching in very wide positions

No. 38
Preparation for playing scales

43

Through all major keys!

1 The arm well guided

2

3 Proceed chromatically

4 Direct the swing always to the pause – the goal!

5

6

7

8 etc.

9 Also chromatically

Proceed chromatically through all major keys – always applying the same (C major) fingering at every stage.

10

Edition Peters 10883

No. 39
Major scales in octaves *)

After all preceding exercises that dealt extensively with the special requirements of the scale – i.e. the smooth passing over and under and flowing change of position – the scales themselves cannot present any difficulties. Memorize the fingerings for the two groups 1–3 and 1–4 – not single fingers – and use different rhythmic patterns and accentuations to vary the exercises. Examples for this follow after the complete chart of the scales. The usefulness of applying dynamic nuances is demonstrated in many practical examples, and can be used to advantage for our exercises: ascending through several octaves a big crescendo, descending a decrescendo; different dynamics for both hands etc.

For the playing of scales the picture of the keyboard must now be subdivided in ever recurring identical groups. The higher technical goal to be aimed at is to make the feeling for the fingering correspond with the position and to remember it. This is the only way to get the scales flowing evenly, not the observation of individual fingers – (provided the basis is solid)!

More advanced students are advised to study scales after the following pattern. From every tone 6 scales accordingly:

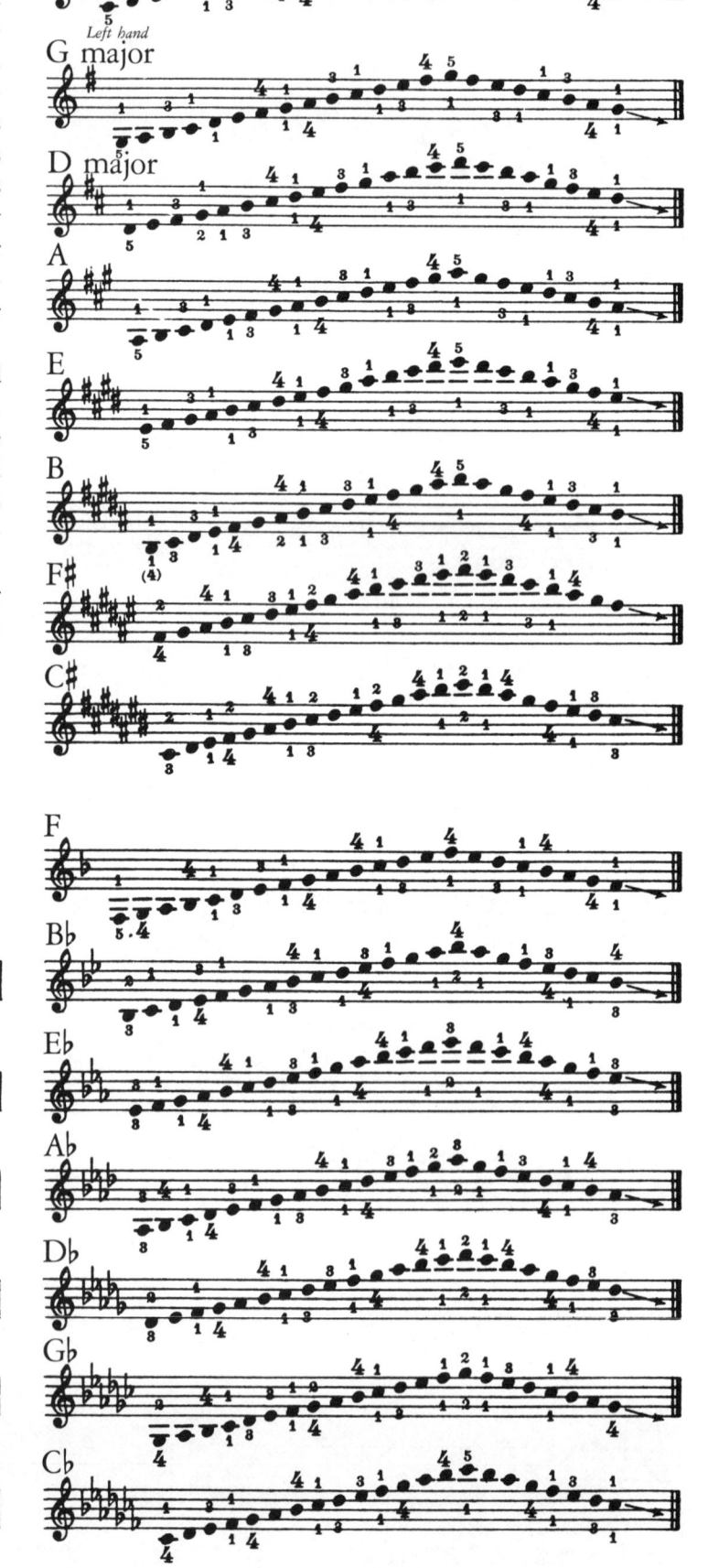

Natural C major

Natural c minor

Harmonic C major

Harmonic c minor

Melodic C major

Melodic c minor

*) All scales to be played through 2, 3 and 4 octaves, with changing rhythm.

Minor scales in octaves
(relative keys to the previous)

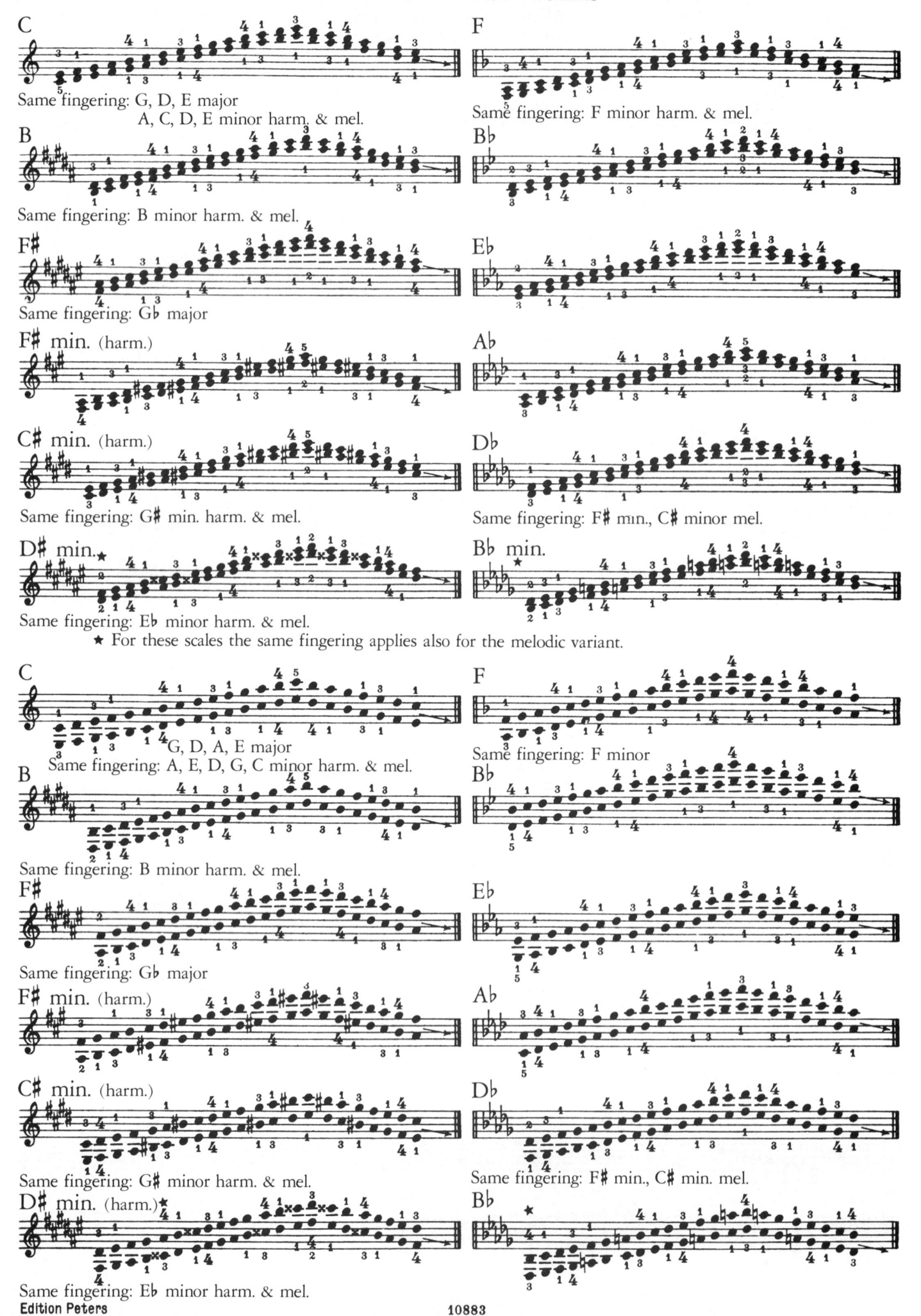

The scales in thirds and sixths

Scales in contrary motion, starting in unison

C

Same fingering: G, D, A, E major
A, E, D, G, C minor harm. & mel.

F

Same fingering: F minor harm. & mel.

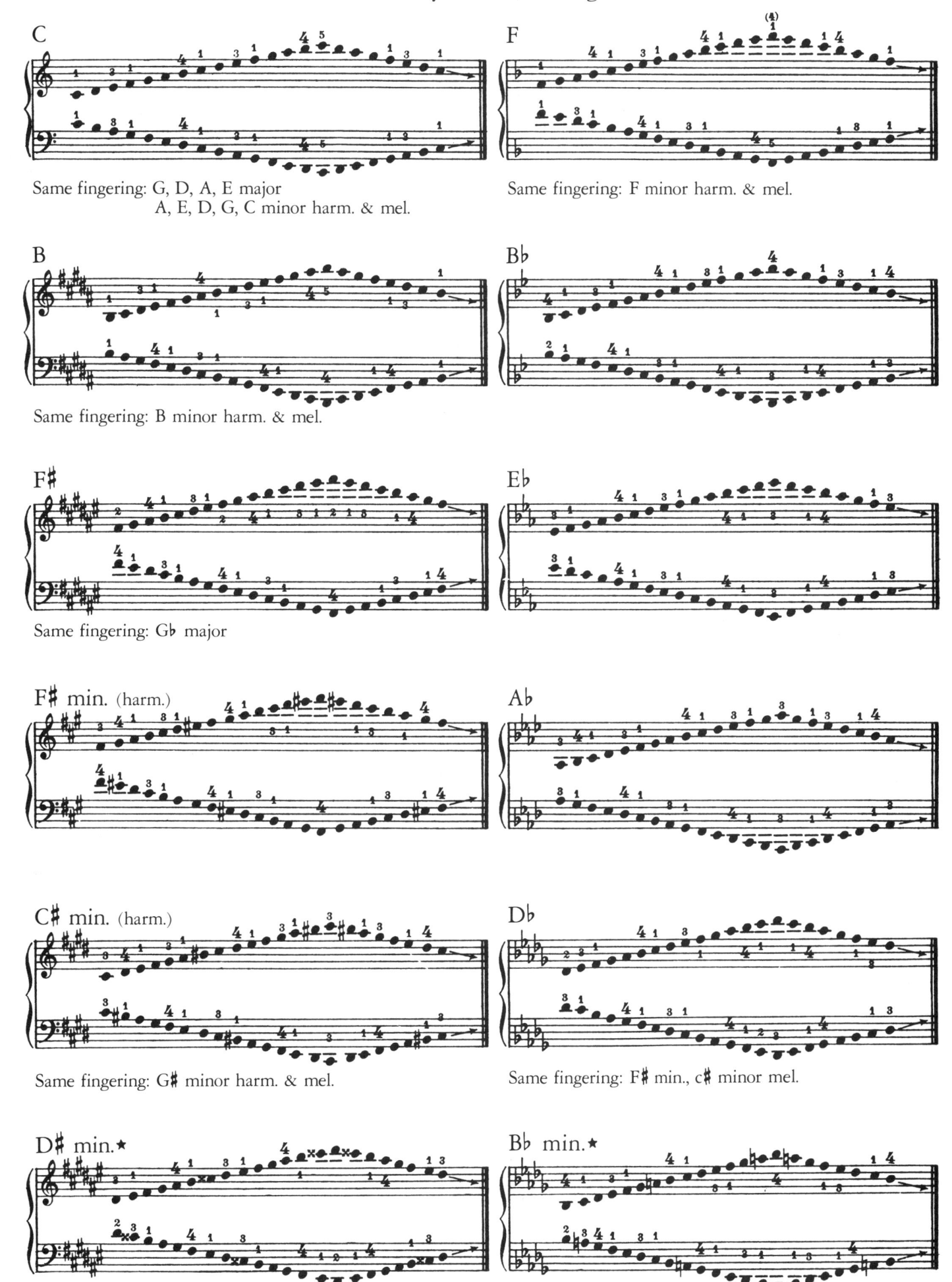

B

Same fingering: B minor harm. & mel.

B♭

F♯

Same fingering: G♭ major

E♭

F♯ min. (harm.)

A♭

C♯ min. (harm.)

Same fingering: G♯ minor harm. & mel.

D♭

Same fingering: F♯ min., c♯ minor mel.

D♯ min. ★

Same fingering: E♭ minor harm. & mel.

B♭ min. ★

Scales in contrary motion, starting at the third

C

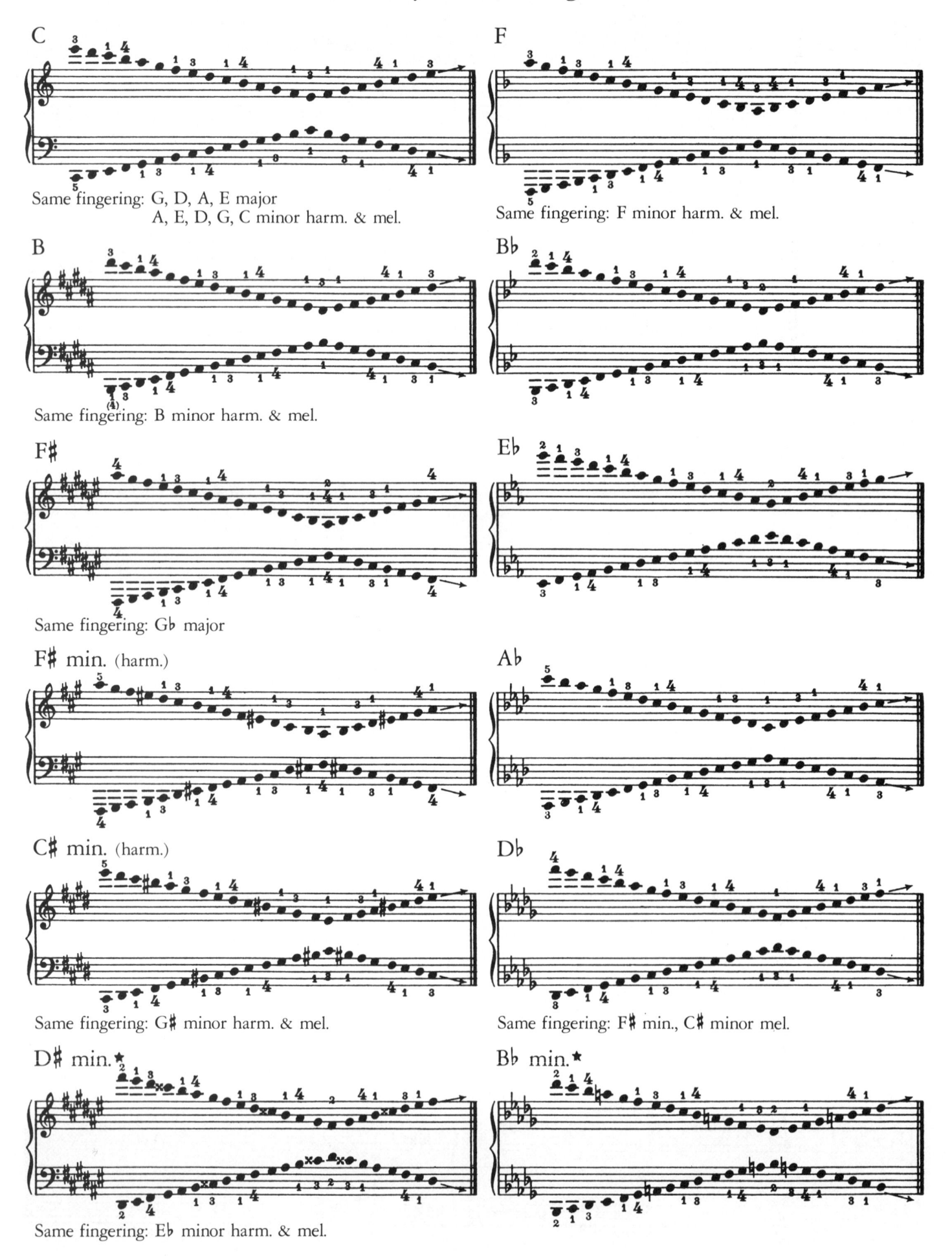

Same fingering: G, D, A, E major
A, E, D, G, C minor harm. & mel.

F

Same fingering: F minor harm. & mel.

B

Same fingering: B minor harm. & mel.

B♭

F♯

Same fingering: G♭ major

E♭

F♯ min. (harm.)

A♭

C♯ min. (harm.)

Same fingering: G♯ minor harm. & mel.

D♭

Same fingering: F♯ min., C♯ minor mel.

D♯ min. ★

Same fingering: E♭ minor harm. & mel.

B♭ min. ★

Scales in contrary motion, starting at the sixth

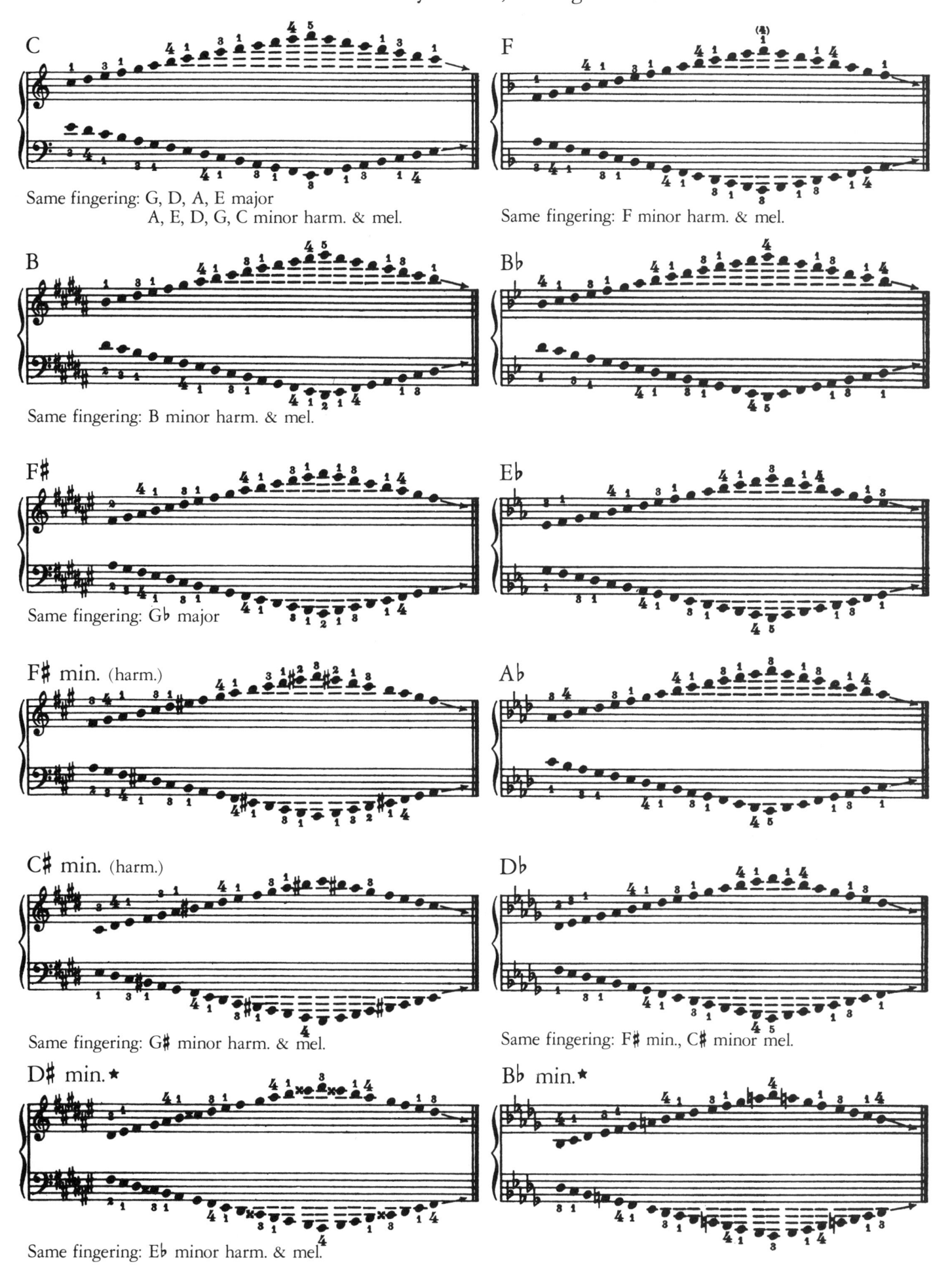

C
Same fingering: G, D, A, E major
A, E, D, G, C minor harm. & mel.

F
Same fingering: F minor harm. & mel.

B
Same fingering: B minor harm. & mel.

B♭

F♯
Same fingering: G♭ major

E♭

F♯ min. (harm.)

A♭

C♯ min. (harm.)
Same fingering: G♯ minor harm. & mel.

D♭
Same fingering: F♯ min., C♯ minor mel.

D♯ min. ★
Same fingering: E♭ minor harm. & mel.

B♭ min. ★

Edition Peters   10883

50

7

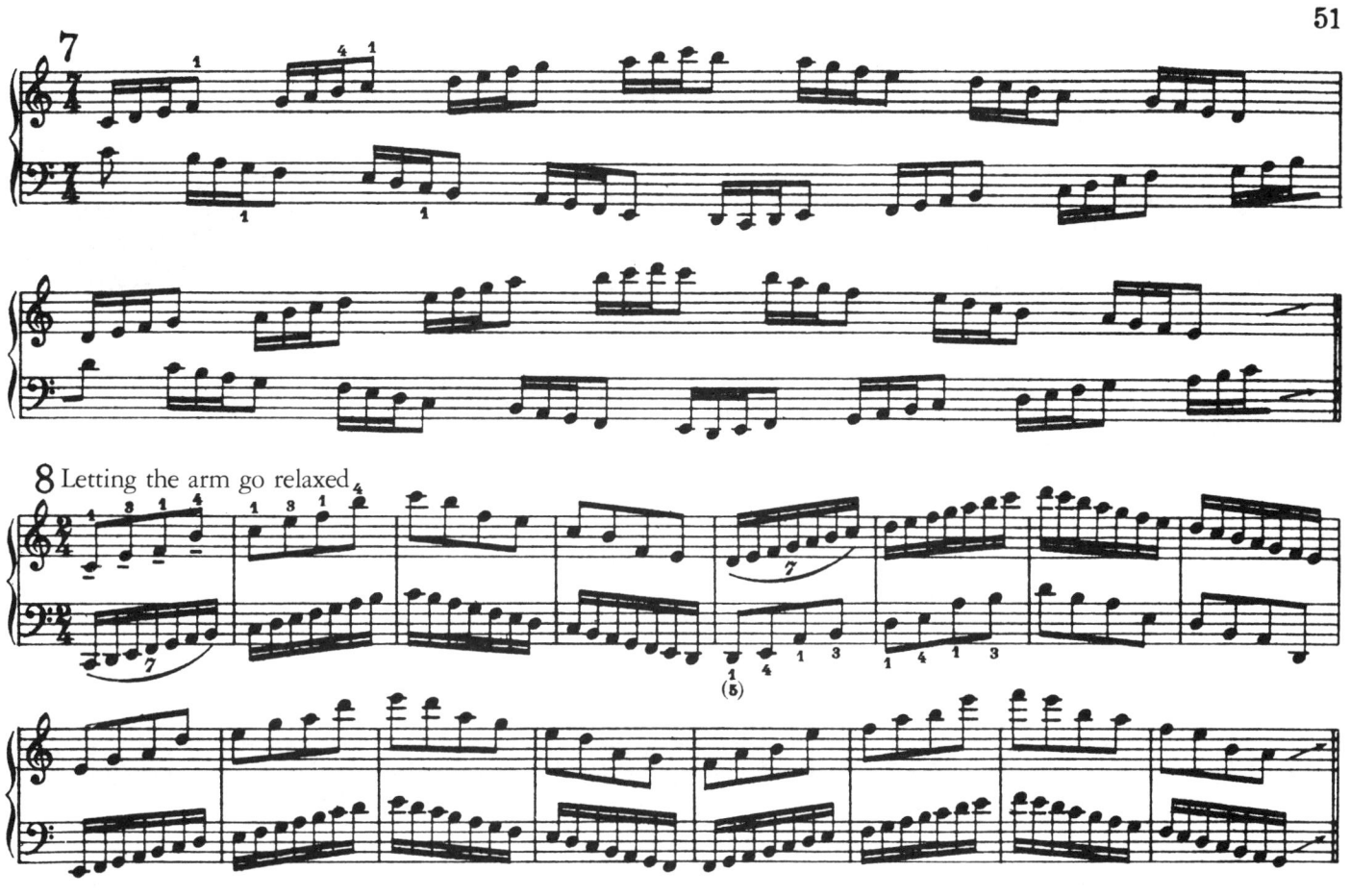

8 Letting the arm go relaxed

Intervals of thirds, sixths or tenths:

9 Help for memorizing the fingerings: Add the missing notes at the beginning and end of the scale in the hand that does not start on the tonic.

10 e.g.: in thirds

11 in sixths

12 For rhythmic variants add one or more notes as appropriate, e.g.:

13

14

As soon as the fingering is established, it is advisable to turn at any step of the scale, not just at the octave. This prepares for similar examples from compositions.

Also in sixths etc. Vary the rhythm, use triplets, quadruplets, quintuplets, sextuplets etc.; also dotted, syncopated and compound rhythmic structures. As you progress, mix runs in thirds, sixths and tenths – this makes practice more interesting and will lead to little improvisations, a preparation for studies.

No. 40
The chromatic scale

Chromatically in contrary motion: starting from the central notes "D" and "A♭" on the keyboard.

* Initially it is useful to pause slightly whenever the encircled groups ①②③ occur in both hands in order to memorize these landmarks well and then continue to the next group.

Start the contrary motion at all intervals to get well acquainted with all combinations of fingerings.

Preparatory exercise: always extending by one or two notes at the top.

Starting on the other central note

etc.

or the lower octave for the left hand

in minor thirds

in major thirds

in major sixths

in minor sixths

Contrary motion starting in unison

Contrary motion starting from all intervals

The whole tone scale

The whole tone scale is ideal for achieving complete independence from "equal positions". If practised with all combinations of fingerings the scale leads to complete mastery of the keyboard. It thus provides an excellent opportunity to develop the playing of uneven finger and hand positions and to adjust continuously. The positions are nevertheless distributed evenly and easily over the hand – a pleasure for every sensitive player who makes use of this. Divide the scale or arpeggiate it – it will always "lie" comfortably with every fingering.

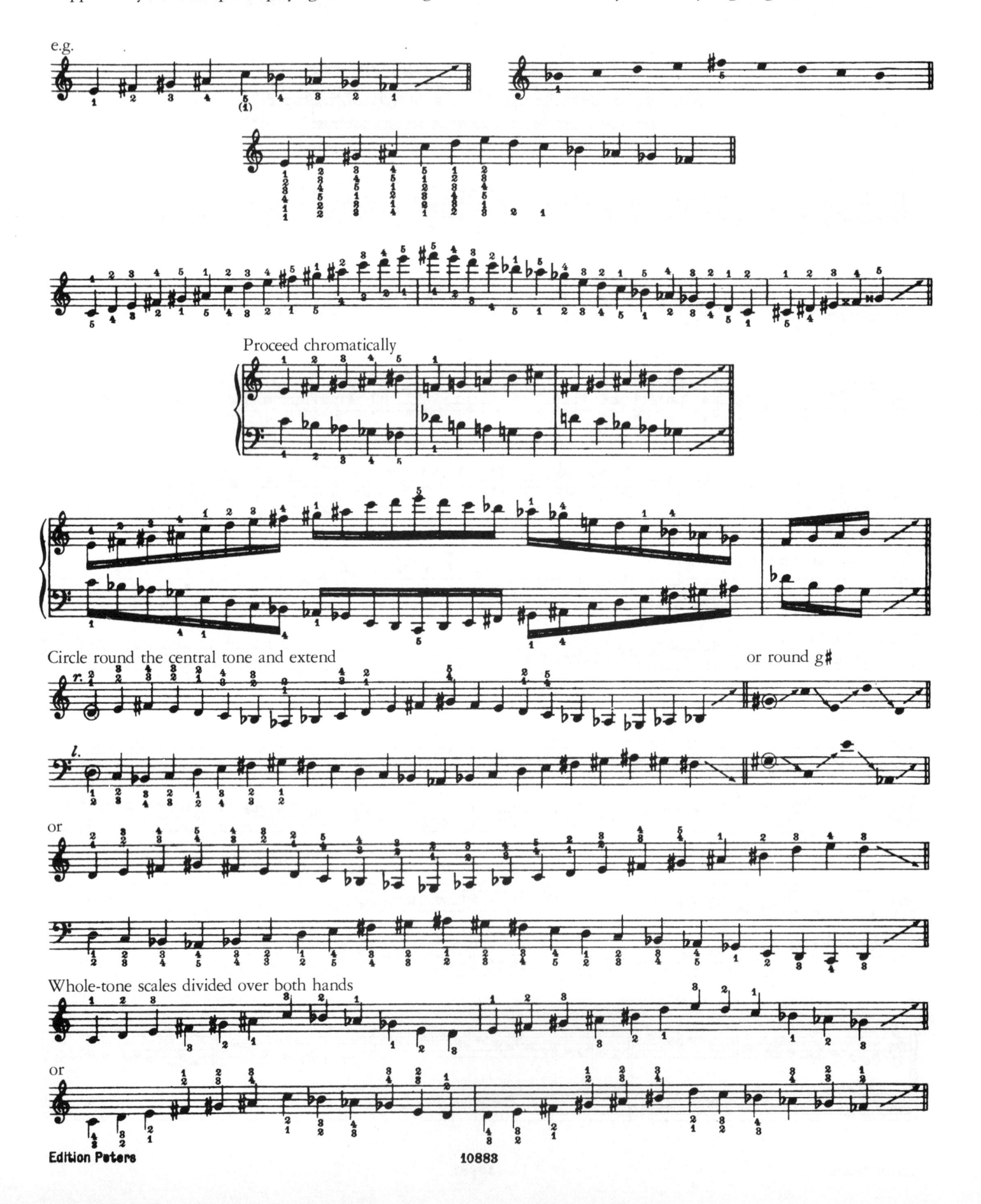

Proceed chromatically

Circle round the central tone and extend — or round g♯

Whole-tone scales divided over both hands

Proceed chromatically

Get the feel of the position in every bar!

Triads

No. 41

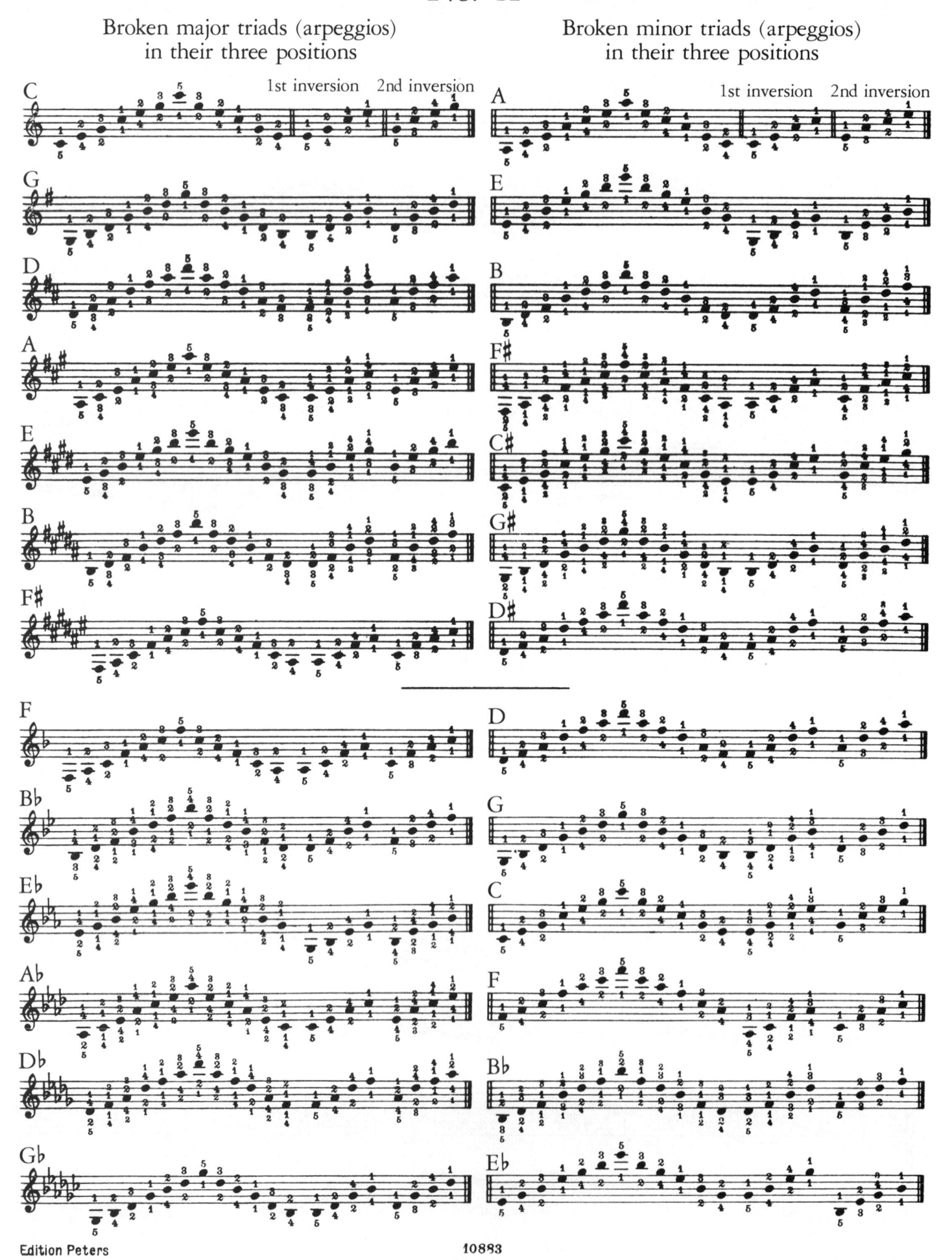

Broken major triads (arpeggios) in their three positions

Broken minor triads (arpeggios) in their three positions

Parallel, starting with the third or the sixth

C

Same fingering: G, F#, Gb major
A, E, D, Eb minor

C

Likewise: G, F#, F, Gb major
A, E, D, Eb minor

D

Same fingering: A, E major

D

Likewise: A, E major

B

B

B min.

B min.

F# min.

Same fingering: C# min., G# minor

F# min.

Likewise: C# min., G# minor

Bb

Same fingering: Eb, Ab, Db major

Bb

Likewise: Eb, Ab, Db major

C min.

Same fingering: G min., F minor

C min.

Likewise: G min., F minor

Bb min.

D min.

Edition Peters 10883

a) In contrary motion from unison

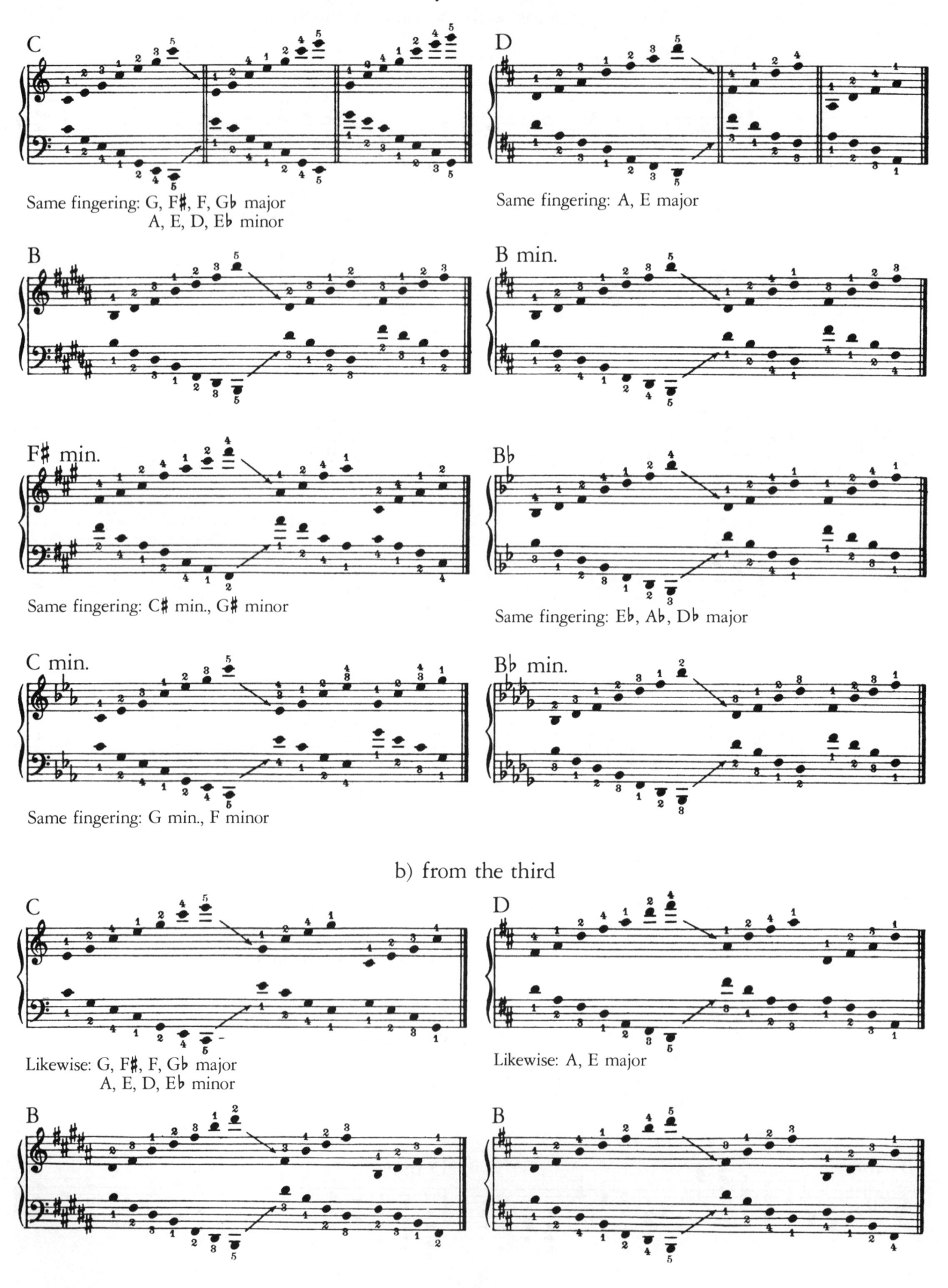

C

Same fingering: G, F♯, F, G♭ major
A, E, D, E♭ minor

D

Same fingering: A, E major

B

B min.

F♯ min.

Same fingering: C♯ min., G♯ minor

B♭

Same fingering: E♭, A♭, D♭ major

C min.

Same fingering: G min., F minor

B♭ min.

b) from the third

C

Likewise: G, F♯, F, G♭ major
A, E, D, E♭ minor

D

Likewise: A, E major

B

B

F# min.

Likewise: C# min., G# minor

Bb

Likewise: Eb, Ab, Db major

C min.

Likewise: G min., F minor

Bb min.

c) from the sixth

C

Same fingering: G, F#, F, Gb major
A, E, D, Eb minor

D

Same fingering: A, E major

B

B min.

F# min.

Same fingering: C# min., G# minor

Bb

Same fingering: Eb, Ab, Db major

C min.

Same fingering: G min., F minor

Bb min.

Variants

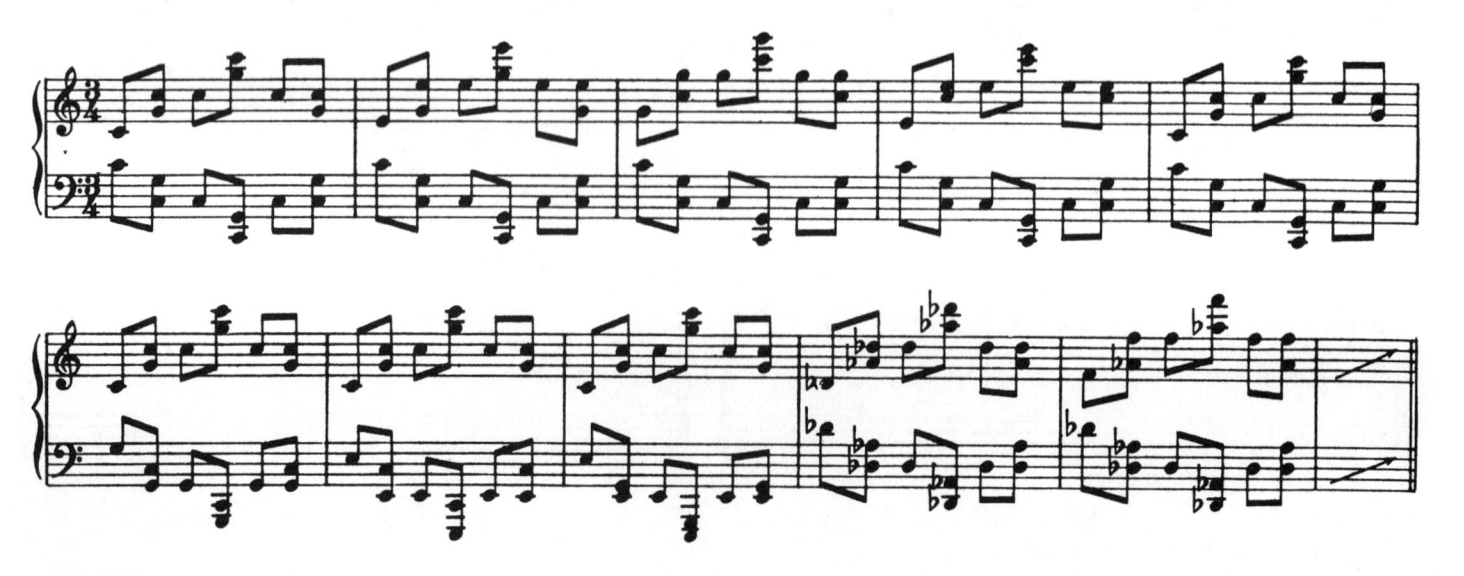

left: inversion

Shift the longer note values also on to the other fingers

It is highly recommended to practise the following arpeggios; play them in such a way that the thumb is used on the black notes, even if it is more comfortable to use it on the white. In practice this will often lead to convenient fingerings in context. It is a very good exercise for the thumb as well.

e.g.

Passing under the thumb with intervals!
Good legato!

Combine all positions. Vary the rhythm. Take examples from practice and study them following the pattern, e.g.

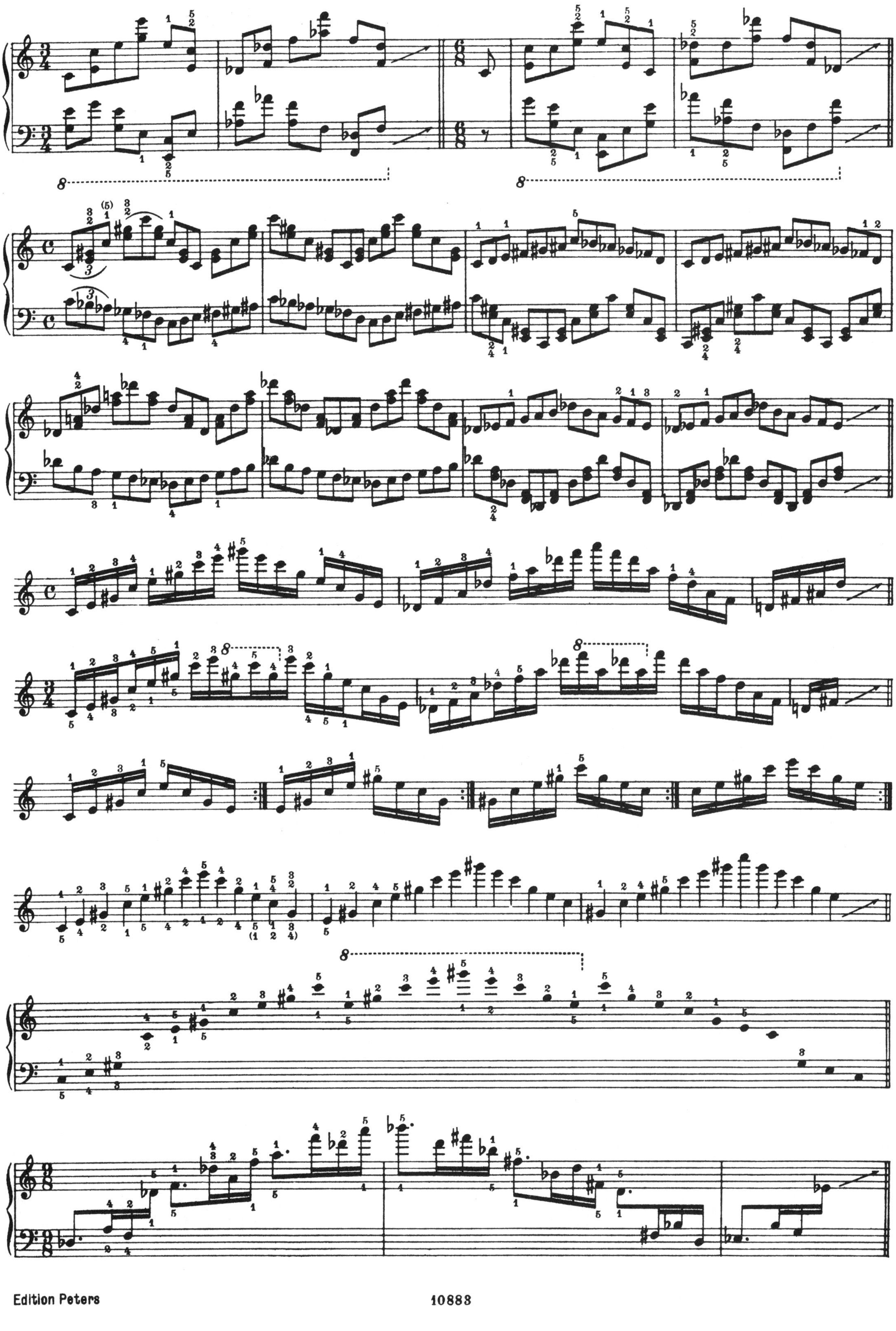

No. 42
Broken diminished seventh chords

a)

a) These first three possibilities cover all others – you will always use the same keys and (if you stick to the correct fingering) even the same combinations regardless with which note you start.

b)

c)

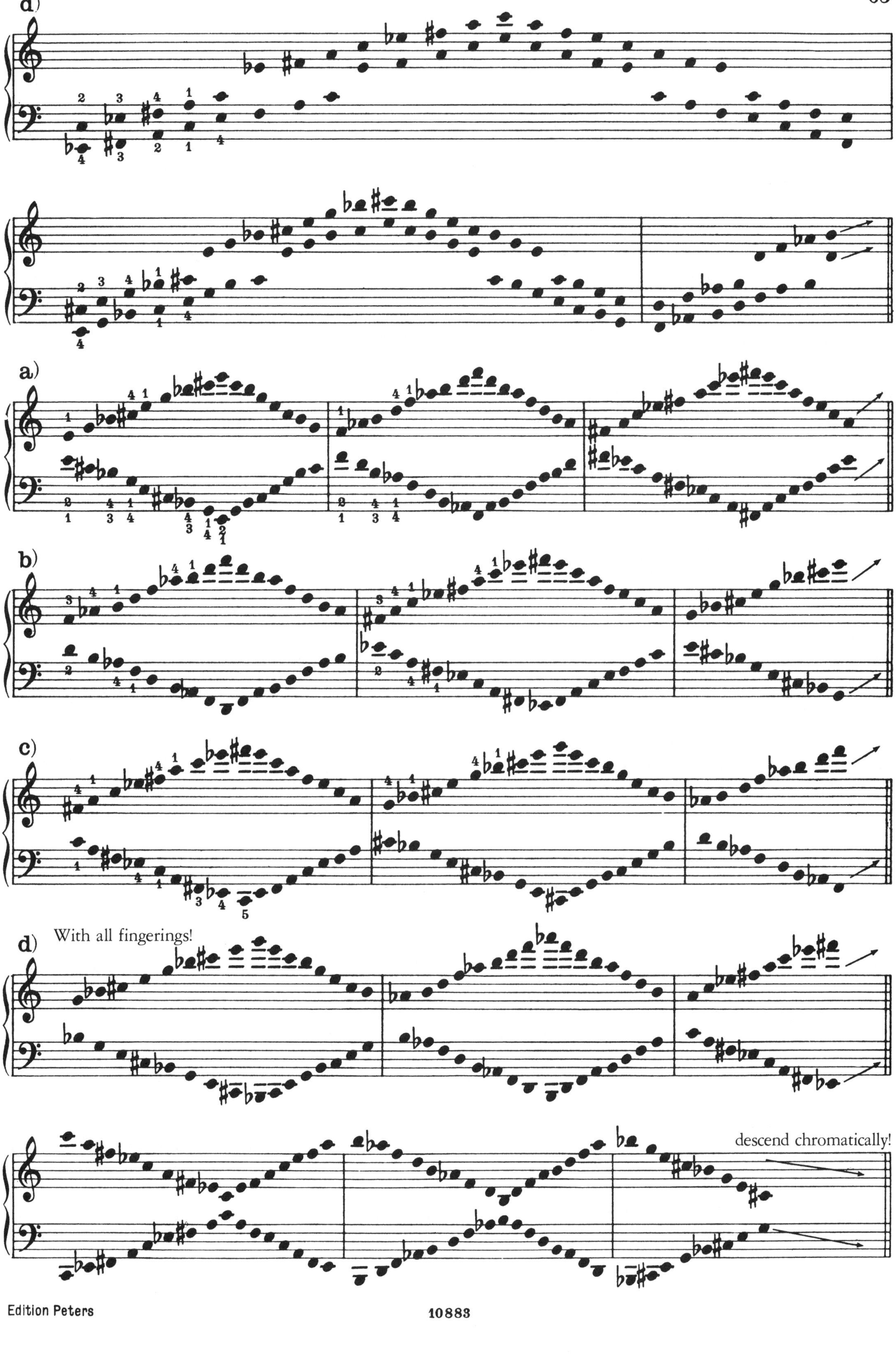
d)
a)
b)
c)
d)
With all fingerings!
descend chromatically!

No. 43

Broken dominant seventh chords

Preparatory exercises

a)
b)
c)
d)
e)
f)
g)

h) left [preparatory exercises: a) – f) inverted]

i) leading notes

Root position — 1st inversion — 2nd inversion — 3rd inversion

Again here without exception all positions must be practised with the same fingering (being concerned about the most convenient fingering only). Practise as extended arpeggios through several octaves.

*) left hand one or two octaves lower

65

ascend chromatically

descend chromatically

Likewise from the basis of the other positions:

etc.

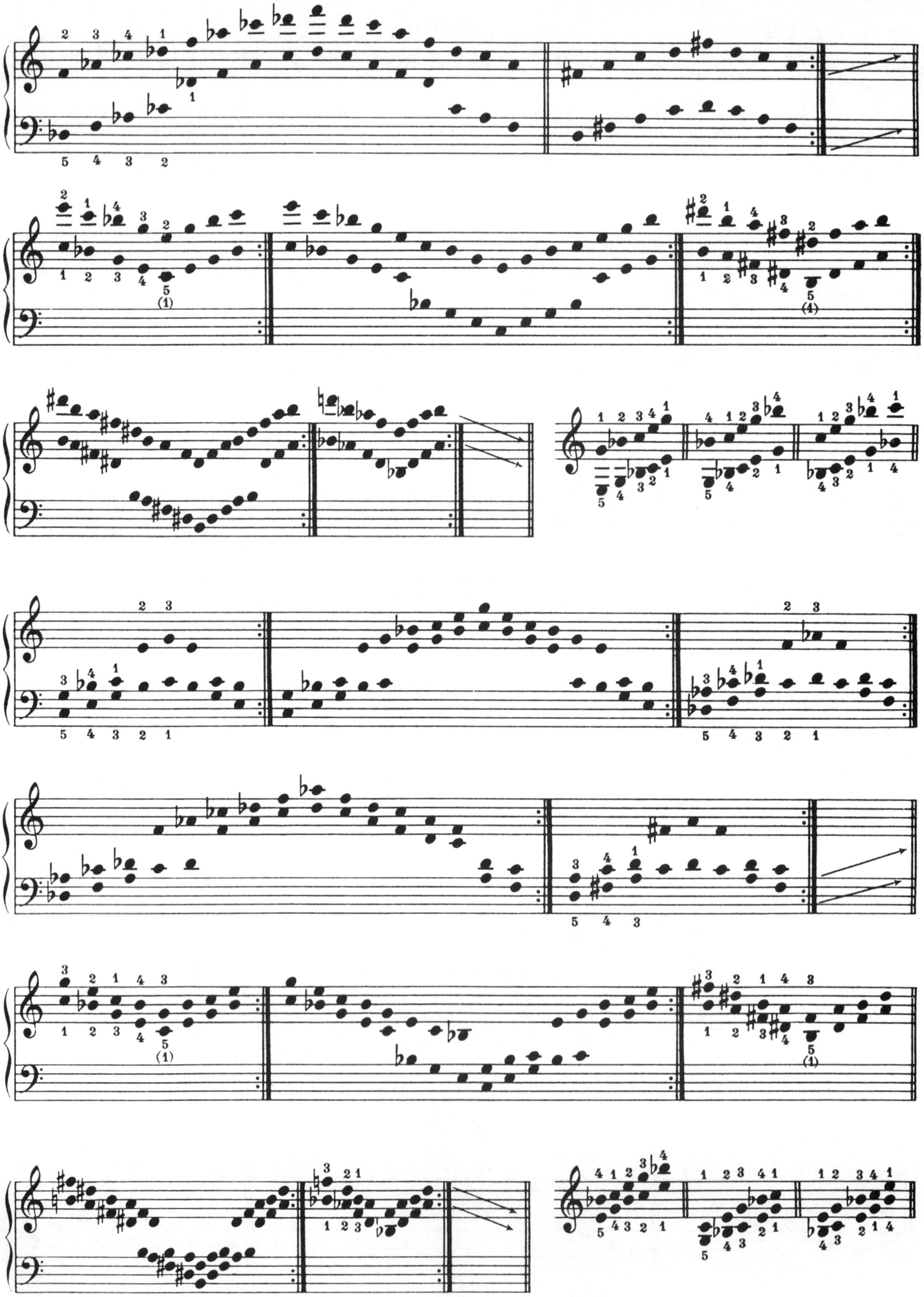

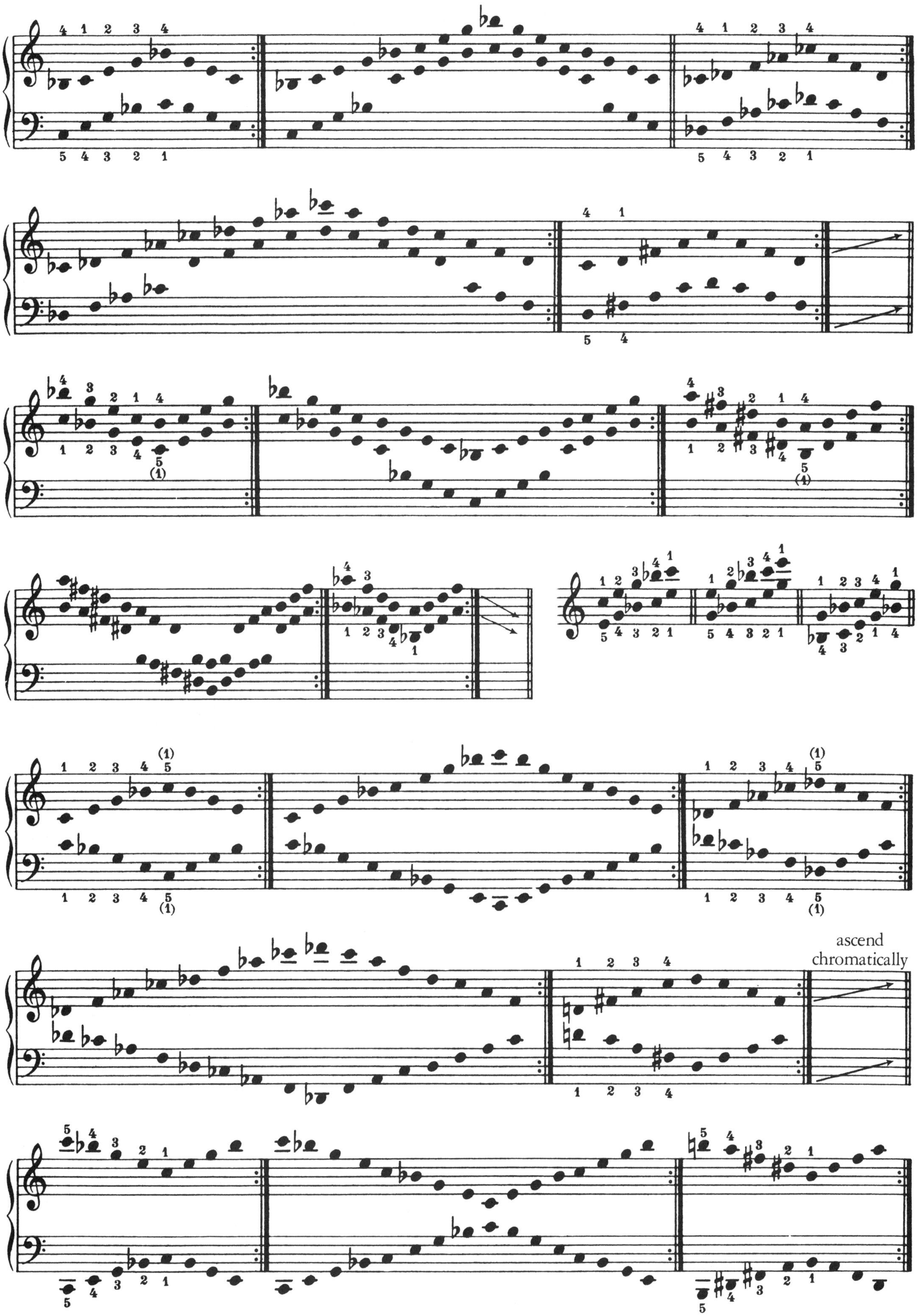
ascend
chromatically

68

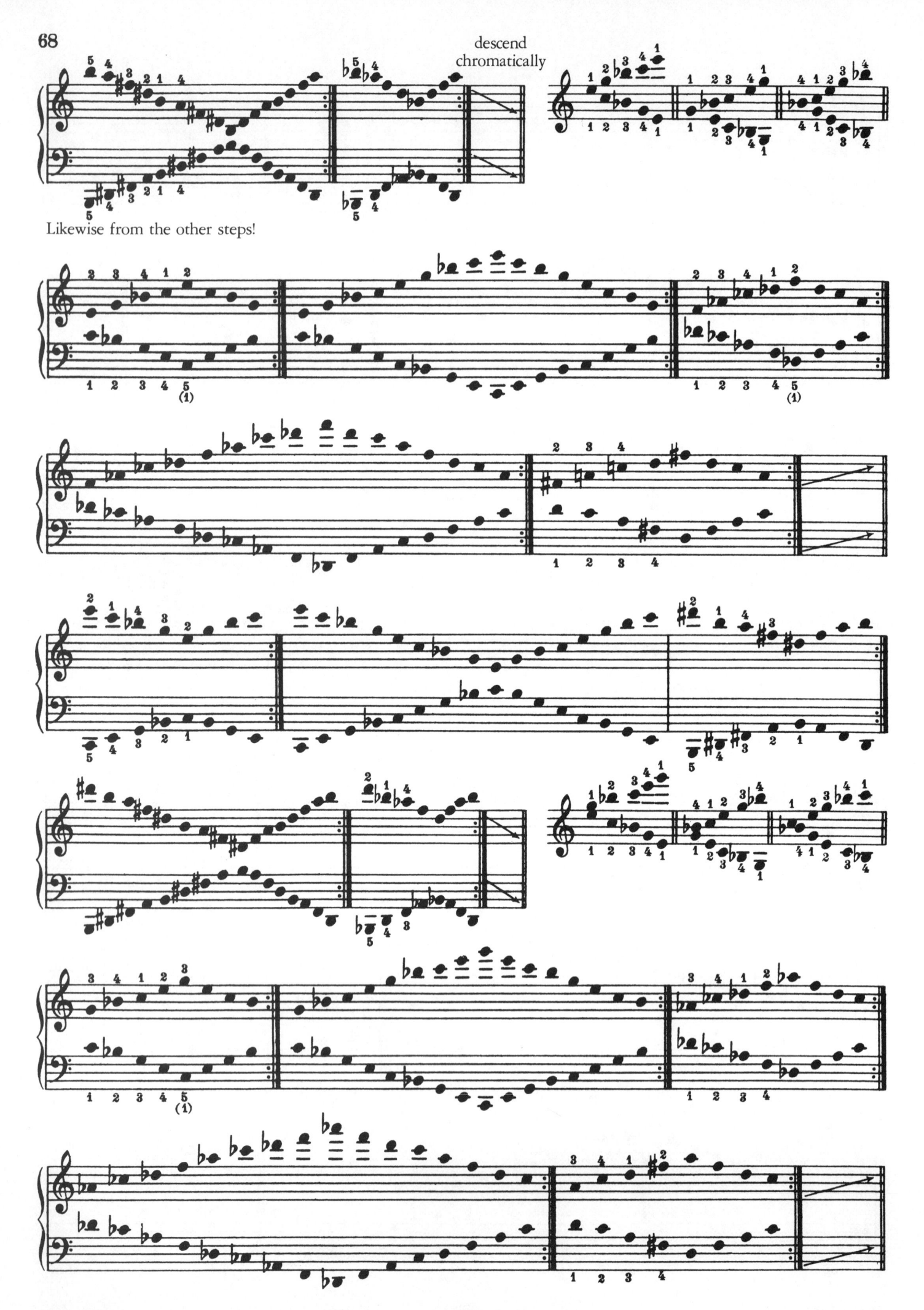

descend chromatically

Likewise from the other steps!

69

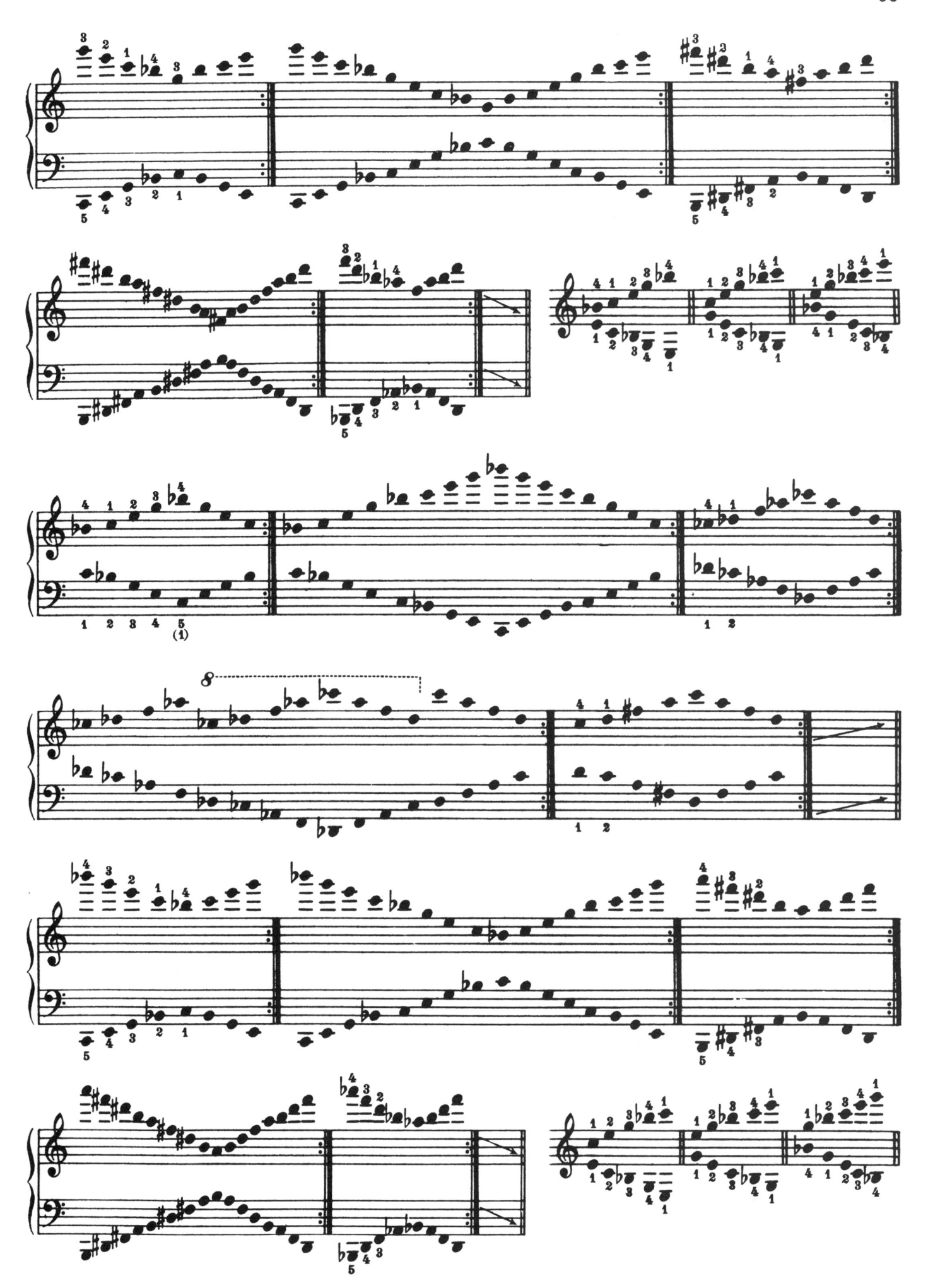

PART THREE
No. 44

Even more useful like this:

	3 2 1 2	3 2 1 2
or	4 3 2 3	4 3 2 3
	5 4 3 4	5 4 3 4

| 3 2 1 | 2 3 2 | 1 2 3 |
| 4 3 2 | 3 4 3 | 2 3 4 | with marked
| 5 4 3 | 4 5 4 | 3 4 5 | accents

>	>	>	>
2 3 4 3	4 3 4 3	4 3 2 3	2 3
1 3 5 3	1 3 5 3	1

1 2 1	2 1 2	1 2 1
1 3 1	3 1 3	1 3 1
2 3 2	3 2 3	2 3 2
2 4 2 etc.

and many more patterns. Excellent training for the whole hand in these purely gymnastical exercises – provided a good finger staccato is observed.

No. 45

Fingering also 2 3 2 3
3 4 3 4
4 5 4 5
1 3 1 3
2 4 2 4

Through all keys

No. 46

Trill for all five fingers

Practise the first six bars until you can play them in a very fast tempo, then continue.

Be careful to get the change of the fingering (★) perfectly smooth and even.

Practise also with $\longleftarrow\longrightarrow$ in each bar or with each trill respectively

M. ♩ = 60–108

72

It might be interesting to know that Mozart favoured this trill exercise.

Thalberg's trill

Trills in chromatic positions and chains of trills

Every position and fingering several times repeated.

After the preparatory exercises of chapters 1 and 2 here are some special fingerings and positions for the trill.

Or doubled. Practise also with change of hands.

Proceed chromatically.

Practise also with the left hand with the appropriate fingering.

No. 47

No. 48
Exercises for the wrist
Detached thirds and sixths

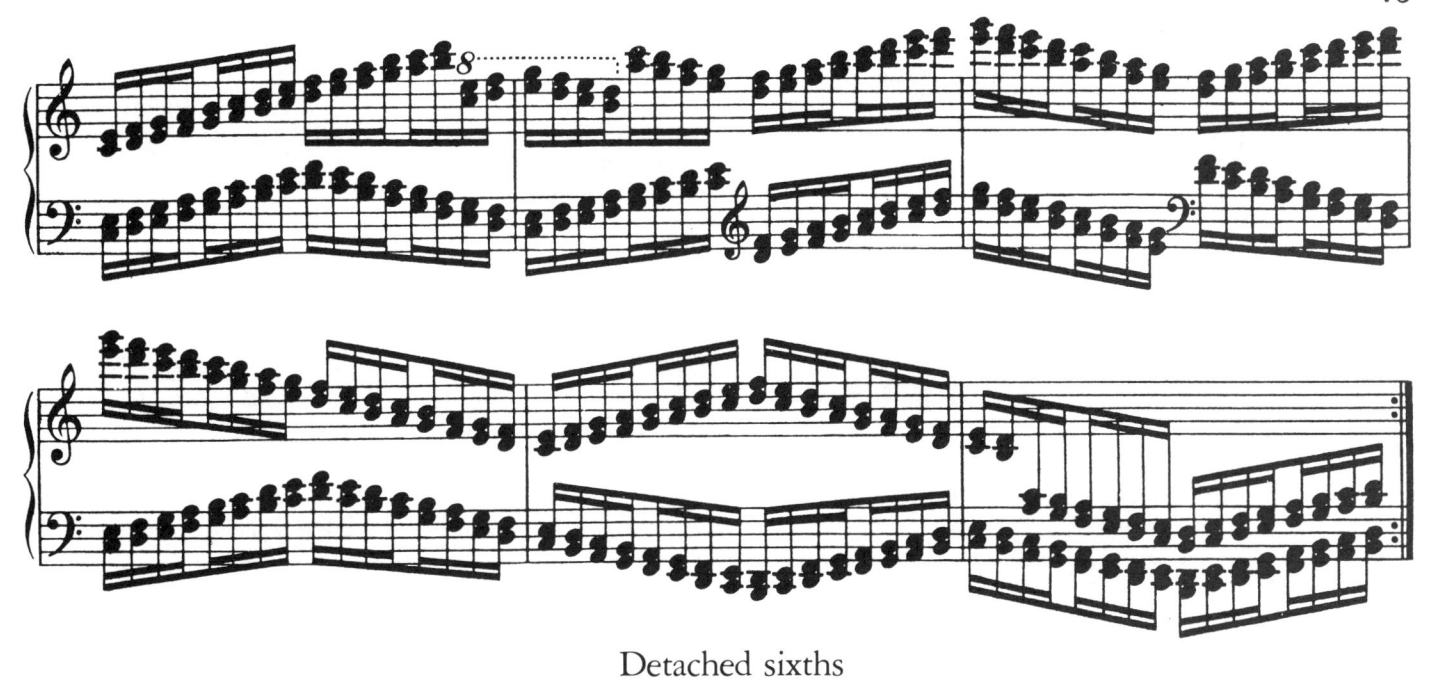

Detached sixths

The comments for thirds apply here as well.

Practise also with $\frac{4}{1}$ and $\frac{5}{2}$ and $\frac{5\ 4\ 5\ 4}{2\ 1\ 2\ 1}$.

M. ♩ = 40–84

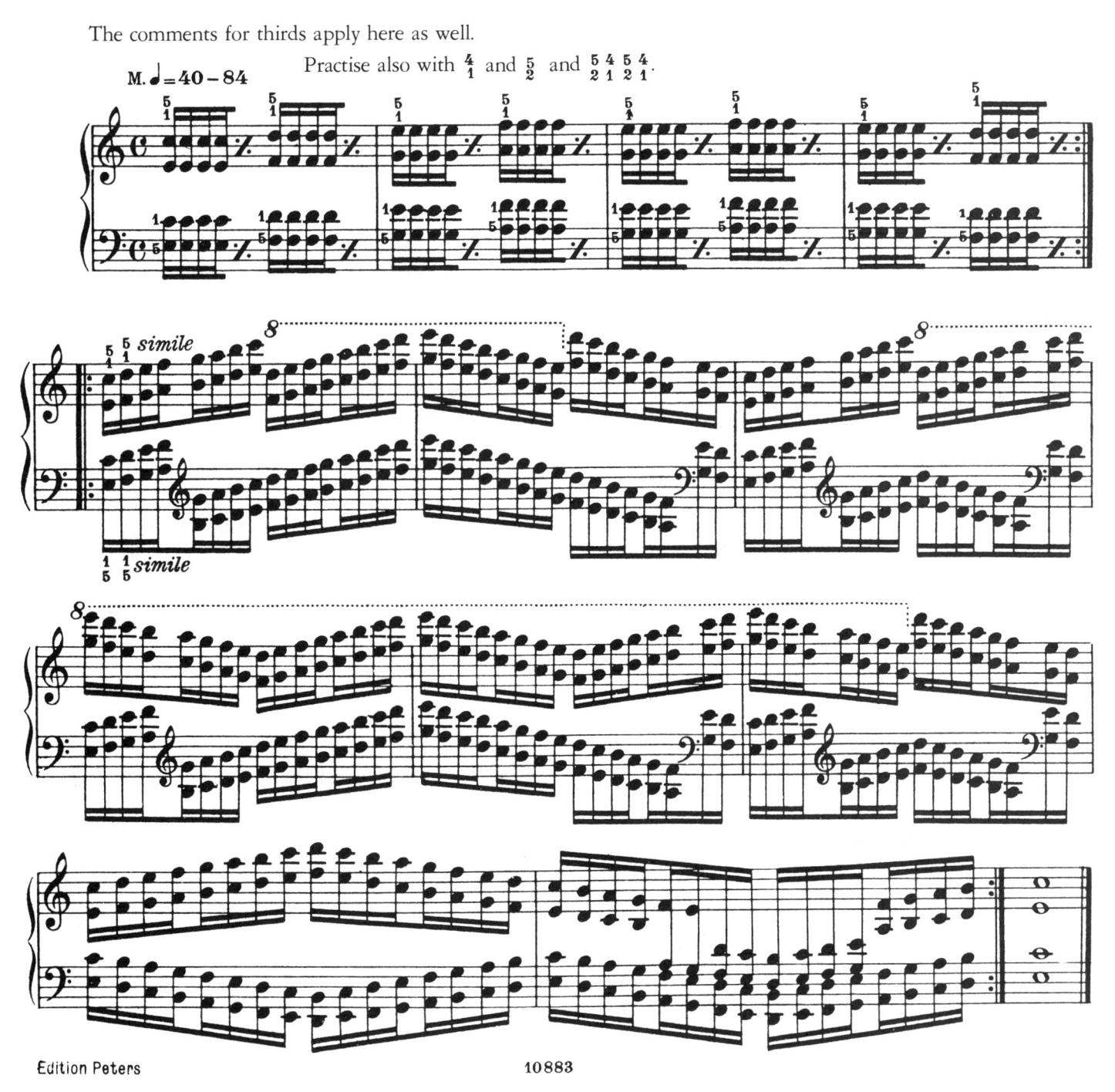

Practise the thirds also with $\begin{smallmatrix}2&2\\1&1\end{smallmatrix}, \begin{smallmatrix}3&3\\1&1\end{smallmatrix}, \begin{smallmatrix}5&5\\3&3\end{smallmatrix}$ and the sixths with $\begin{smallmatrix}4&4\\1&1\end{smallmatrix}$ and $\begin{smallmatrix}5&5\\2&2\end{smallmatrix}$.

Hanon's instruction for this: "Lift the wrists with every note, but keep the arm still", is anatomically impossible. He wants a perfect so-called wrist staccato: the forearm keeps steady and the hand flicks briskly up and down.

Portamento can also be practised with this exercise. The fingers remain on the keys – lift them only slightly when you raise the wrist and let them sink into the depth of the keys again when the forearm drops. Recommended e.g. for smooth and soft accompaniment.

Slowly – without interruption of the tone progression – wrist flexible.

Practise also repetitions and progressions of chords in both styles. No. 60 could accordingly be altered into:

With inserted leaps – staccato and portamento

also in transposition through several octaves

No. 49

Extension between the first and fourth and between the second and fifth fingers of each hand. (This exercise is very useful to gain independence of the fingers.)

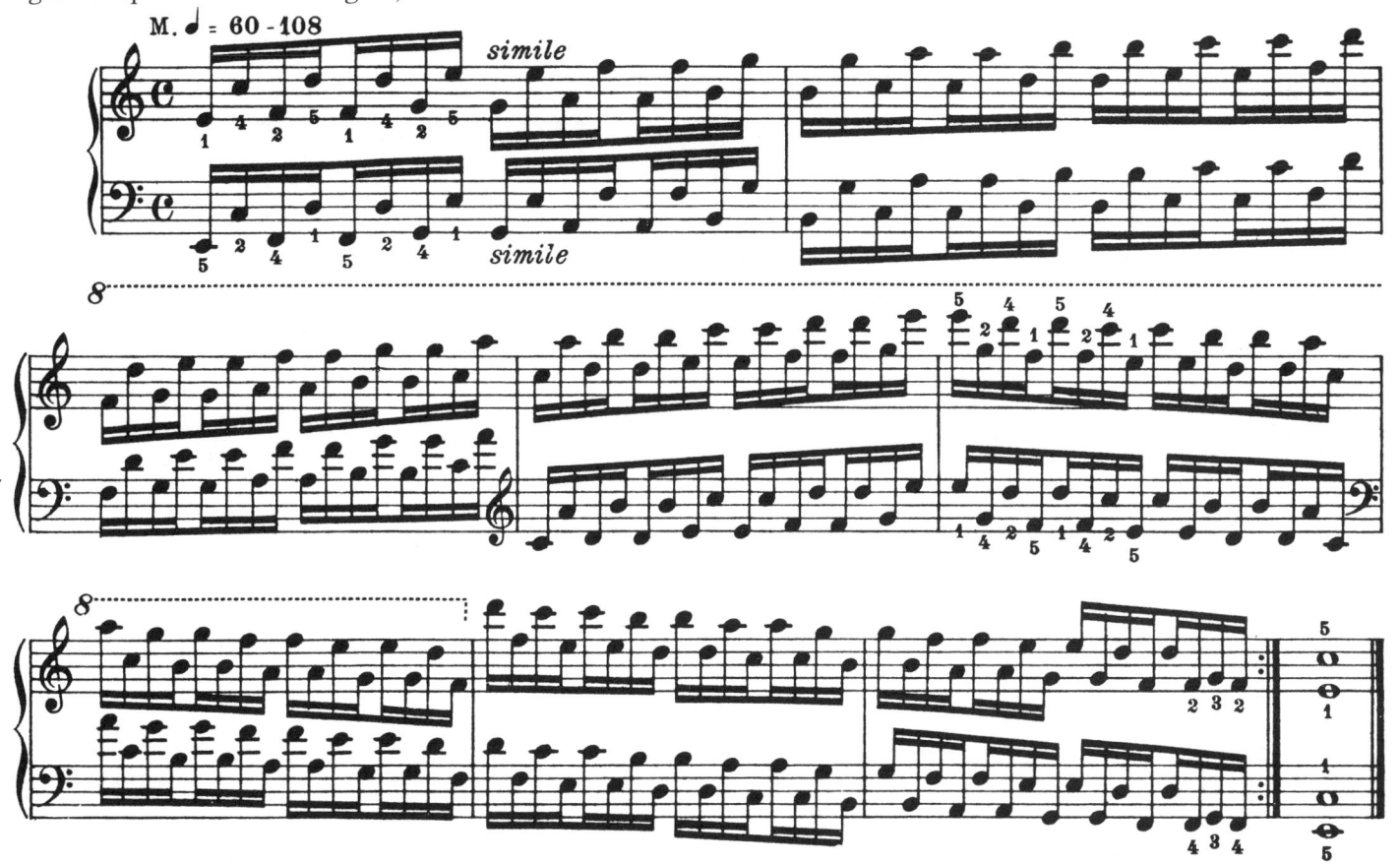

Can be played with very light movement of the fingers (leggiero) or with small flinging or shaking movements of the arm. Very fast tempo!

Also inversion of the figure – thus the 4th and 5th fingers will be emphasized. The hand helps with small flinging and shaking movements. Widening of the intervals is useful.

No. 50
Parallel thirds

Start heavily with sagging finger-tips, later lightly and quickly.

The change of fingers at 1) must be helped most delicately by a soft rising and sinking of the wrist.

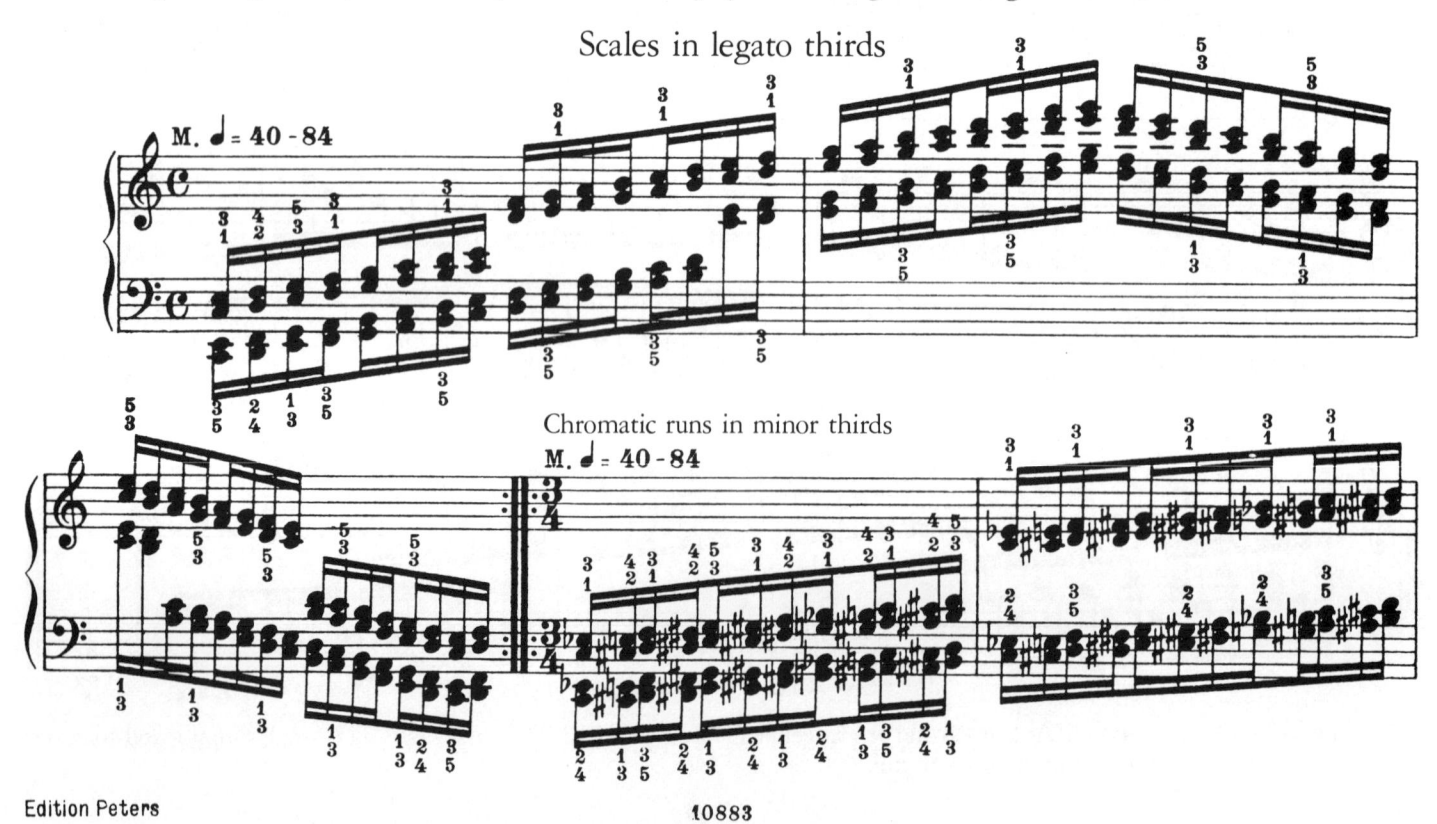

All major keys

Scales in legato thirds

Chromatic runs in minor thirds

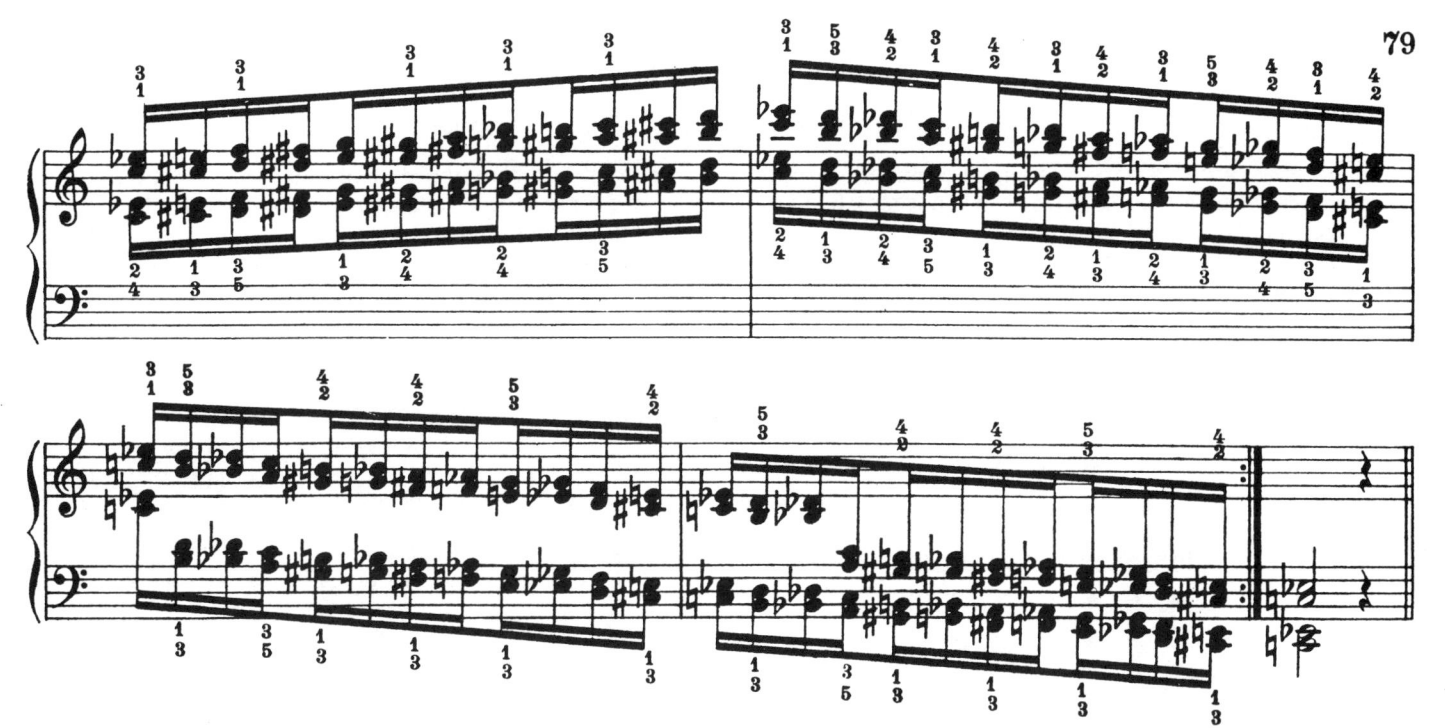

Do not try to simplify the change from $\frac{3}{1}$ to $\frac{5}{3}$ by releasing the 3rd finger too soon. Instead help with a flexible wrist by suddenly swinging or better gliding without actually losing contact with the keys – likewise for the change $\frac{2}{1}$.

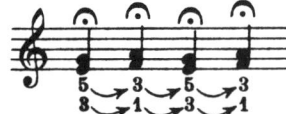

Long pause on the third, then perform the swing suddenly and quickly and pause again until the next swing.

Chromatic major thirds

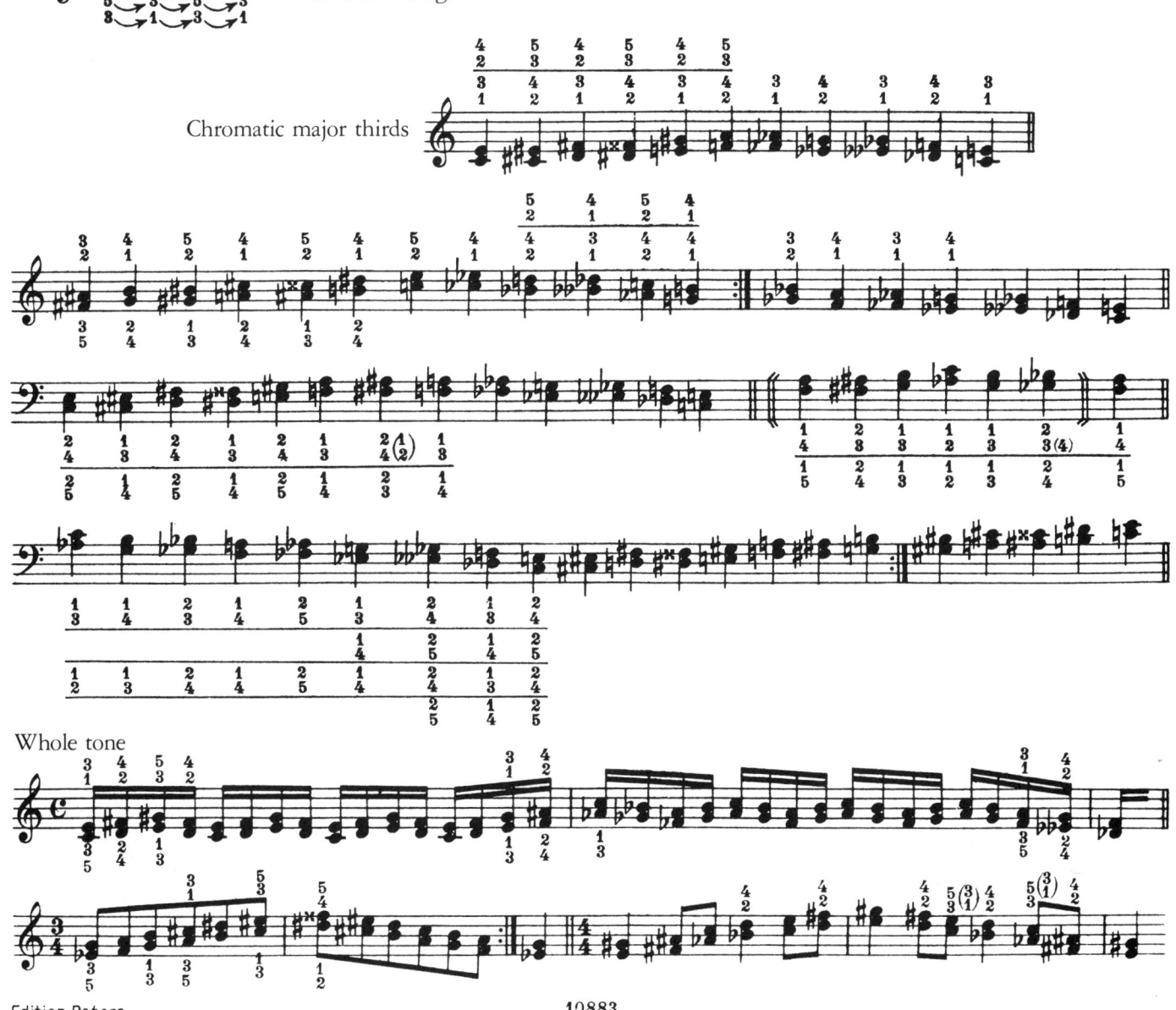

Whole tone

No. 51
Preparatory exercises for runs in octaves

The wrist must always remain flexible, the fingers gripping the octave must rest firmly but not tensely on the keys and slightly bent in the middle.

Different methods of practising octaves: According to context – sound, rhythm, tempo – either a big swinging or a small gliding execution will be required.

In rhythmic runs the end of the swing, or the aim, is always on the longer note or the peak respectively.

For even runs – like the scales in No. 53 – an even and smooth movement is necessary, preferably horizontally and in the manner of a glissando.

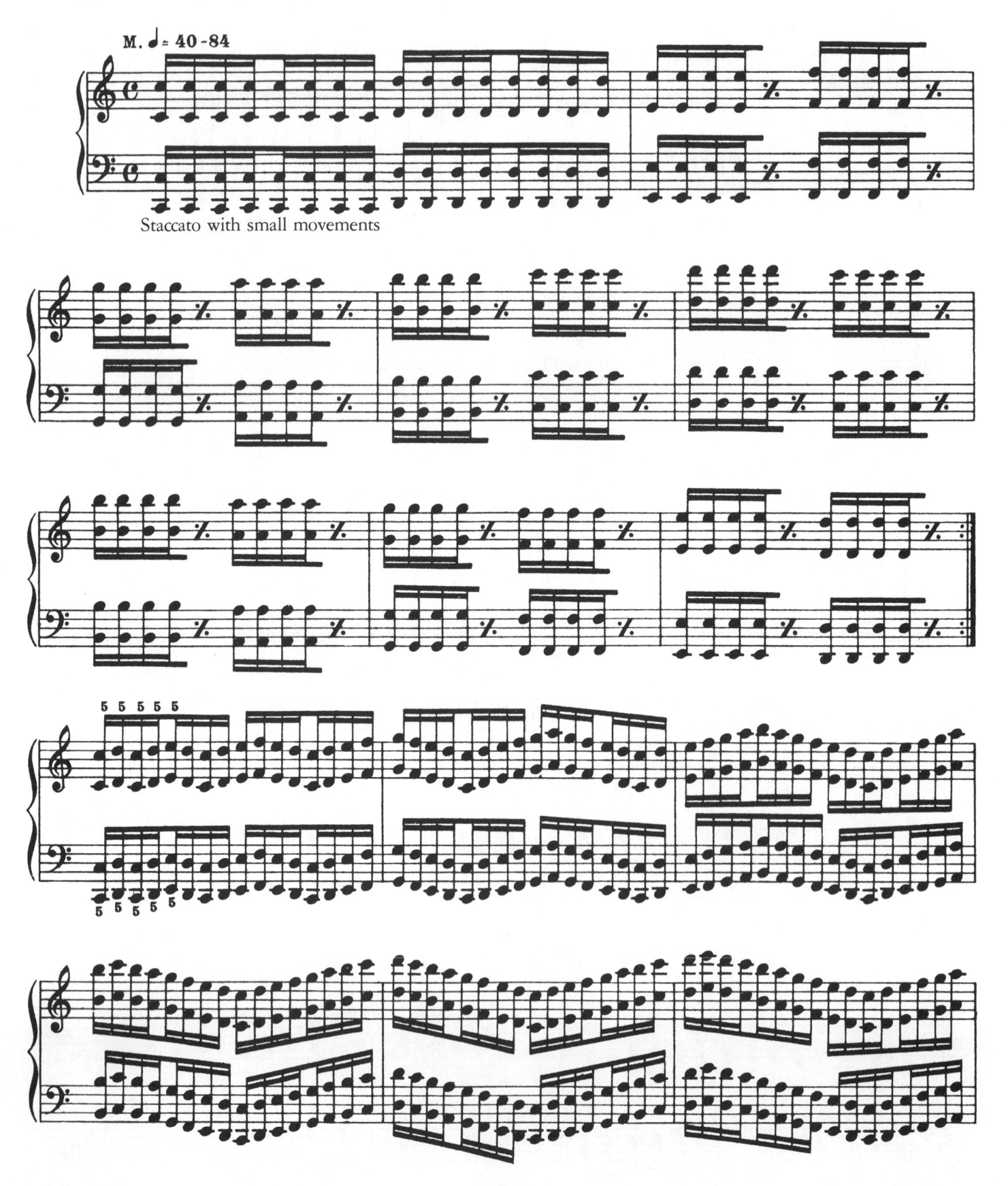

Staccato with small movements

81

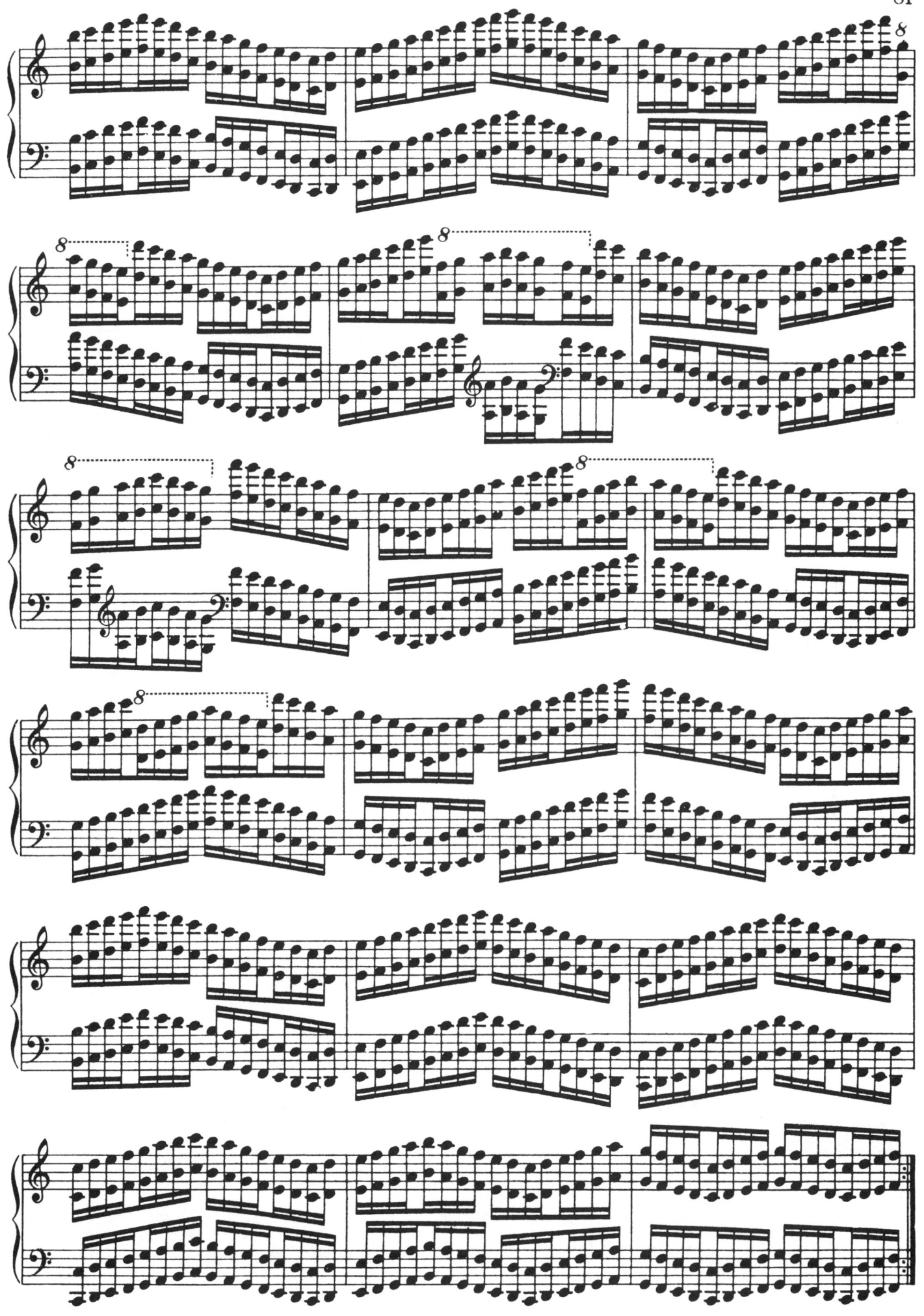

82

No. 52
Major and minor scales in thirds

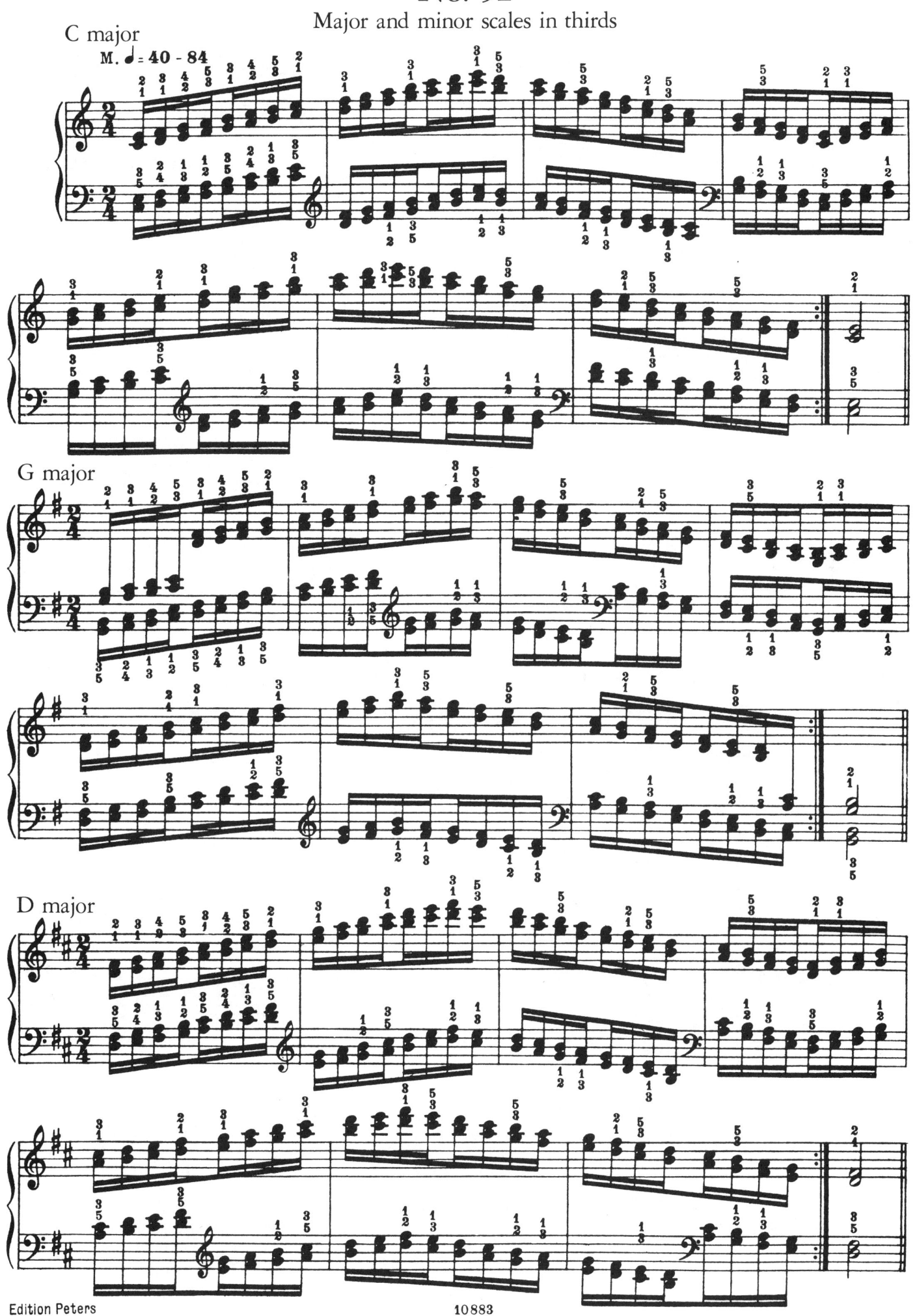

A major

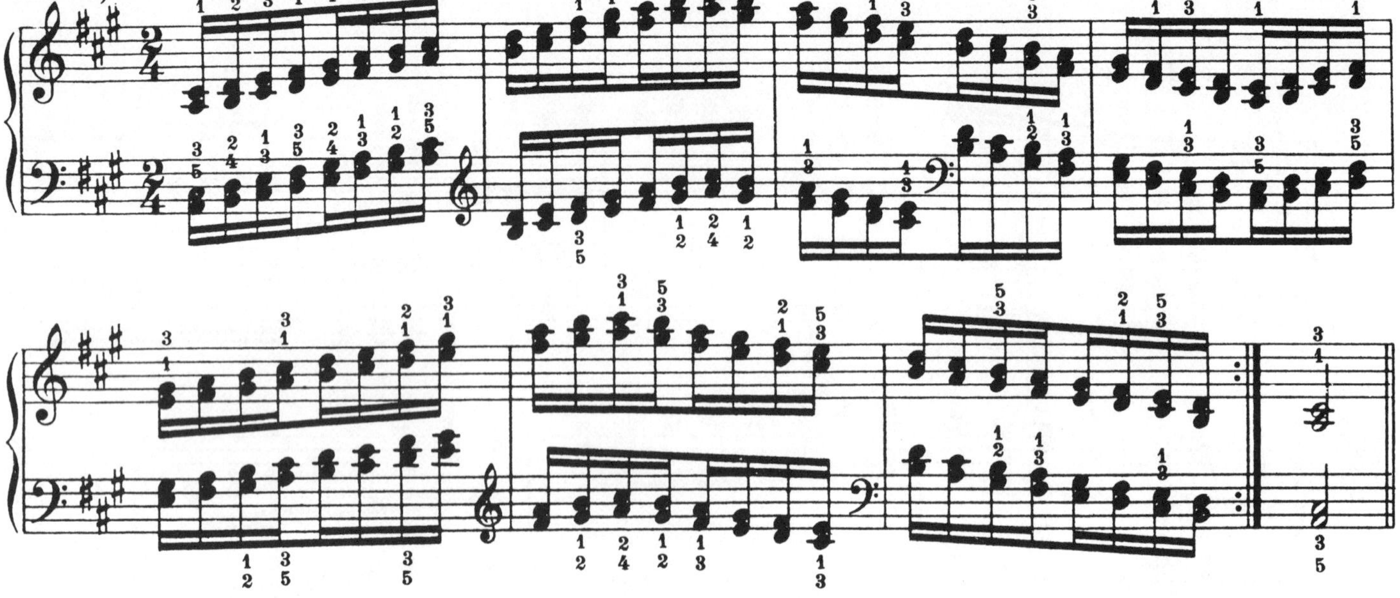

E major

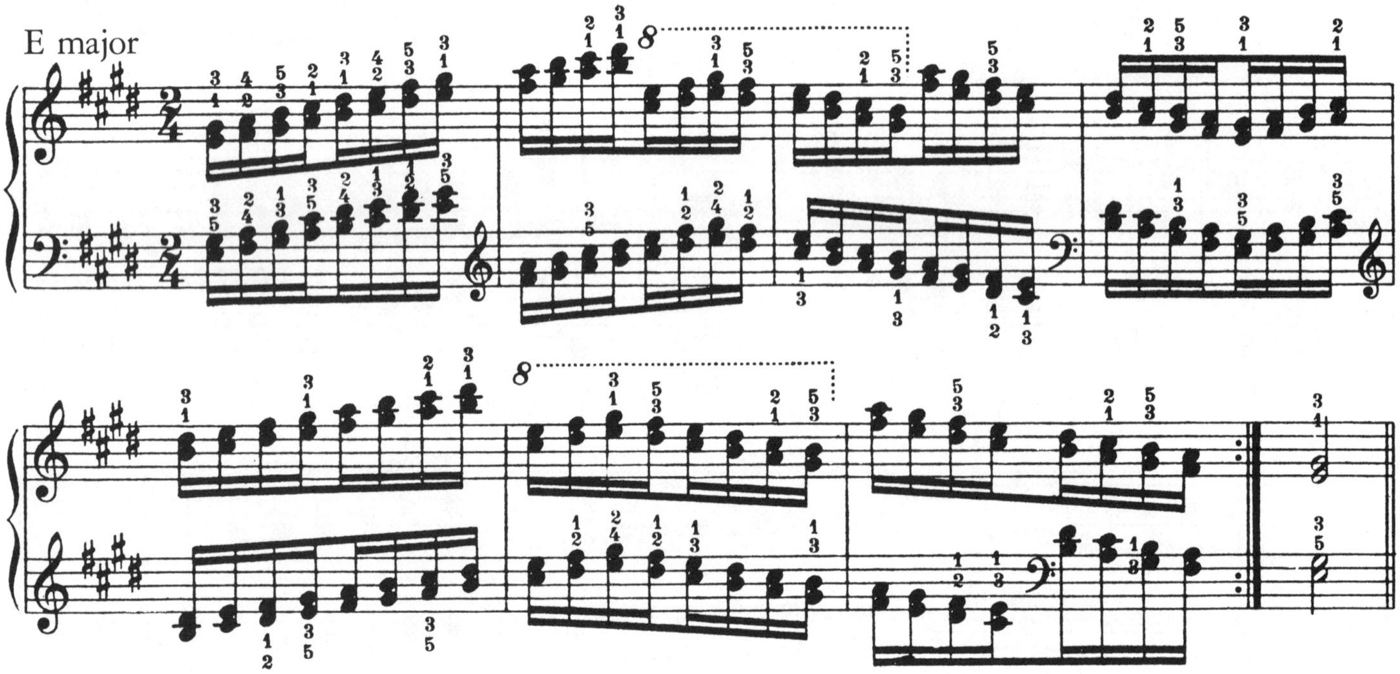

F major

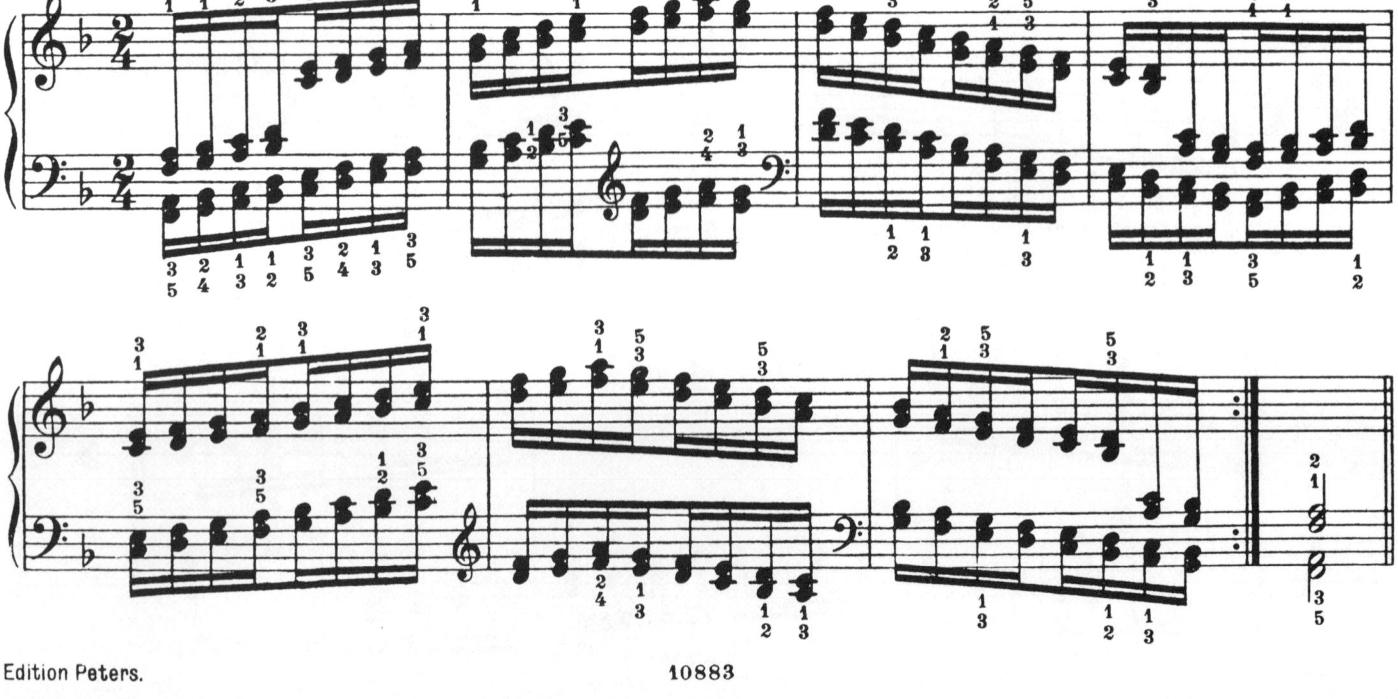

Bb major

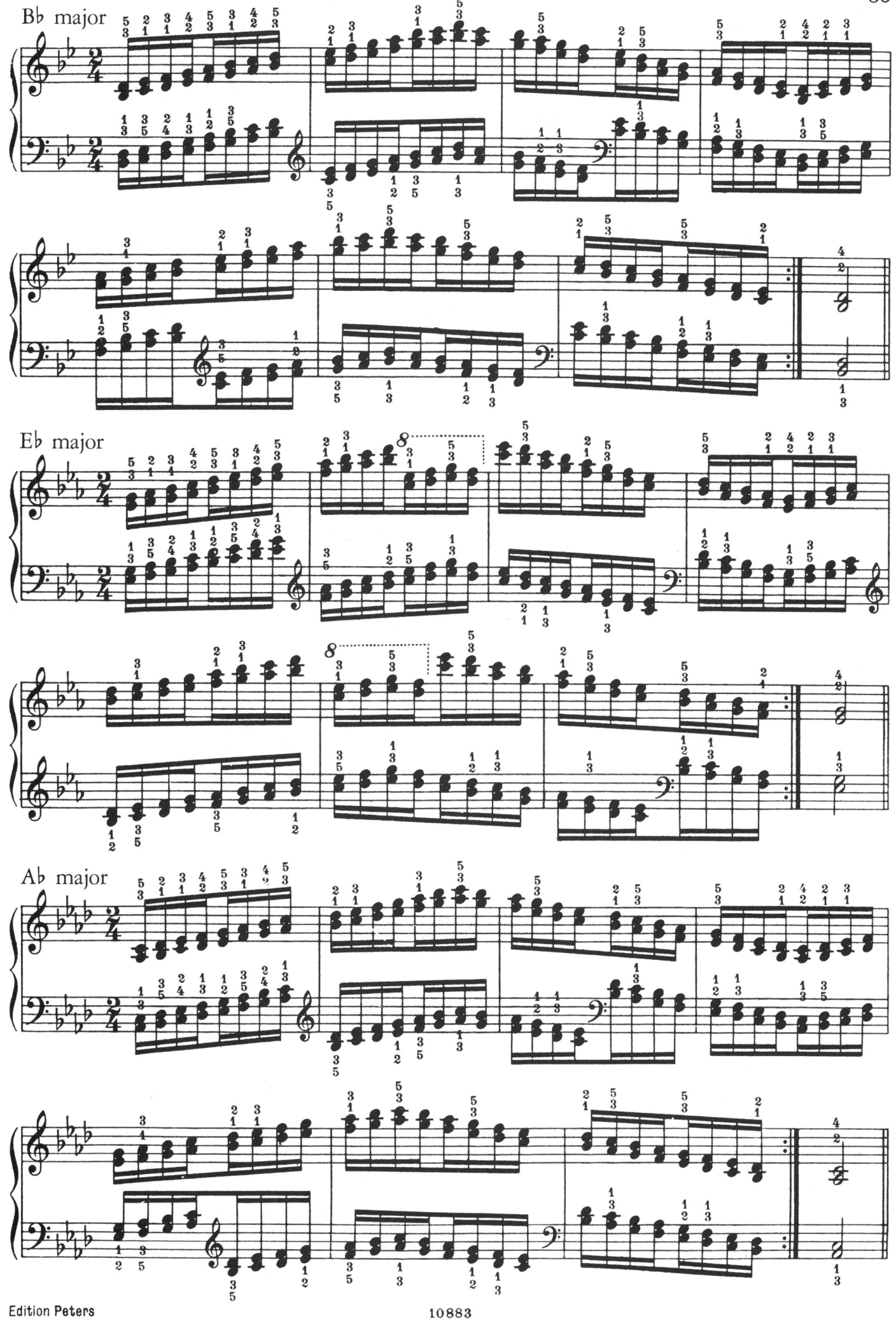

Eb major

Ab major

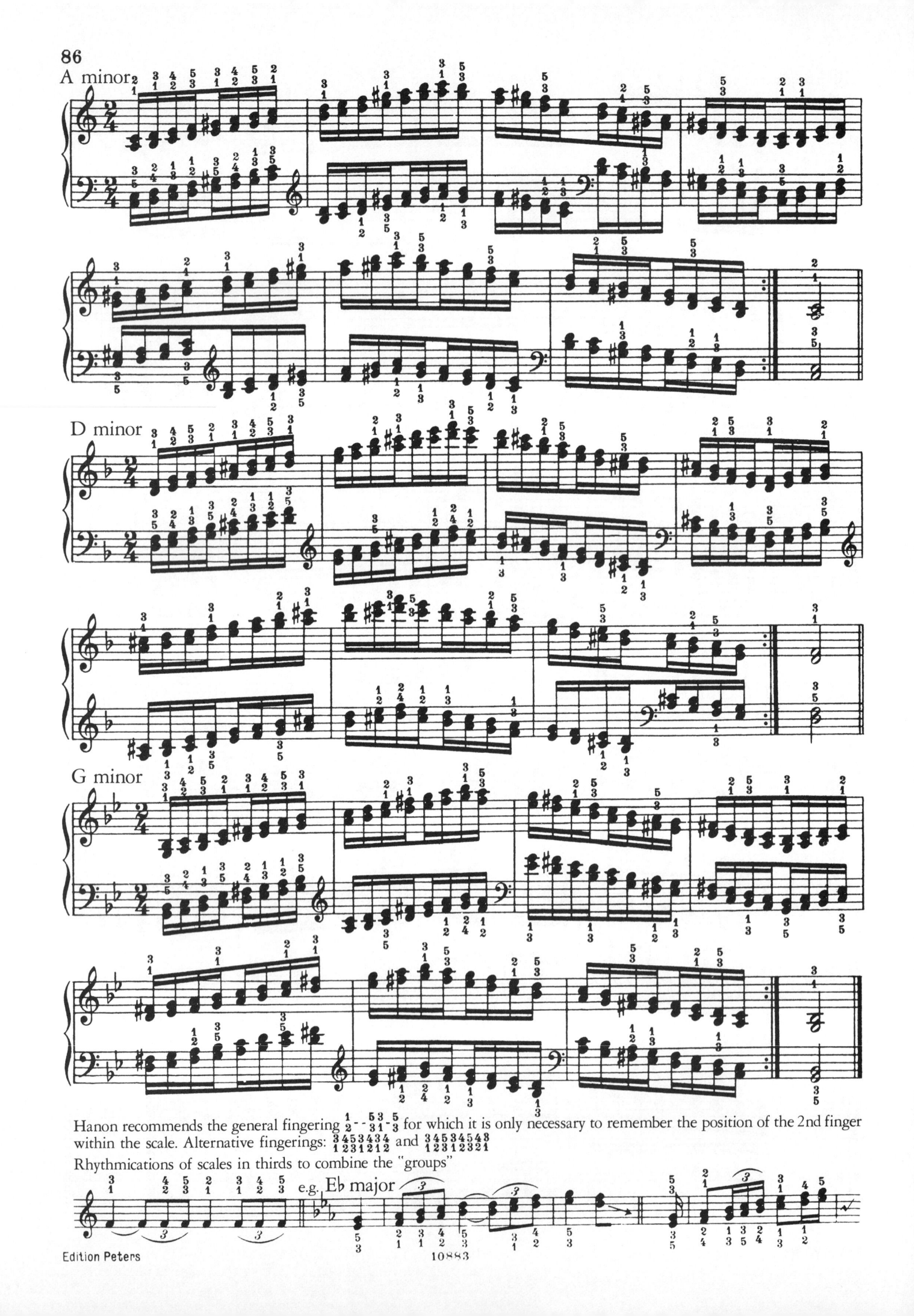

Hanon recommends the general fingering $\genfrac{}{}{0pt}{}{1\ \ 5\ 3\ 5}{2\ \ 3\ 1\ 3}$ for which it is only necessary to remember the position of the 2nd finger within the scale. Alternative fingerings: $\genfrac{}{}{0pt}{}{3453434}{1231212}$ and $\genfrac{}{}{0pt}{}{34534548}{12312321}$

Rhythmications of scales in thirds to combine the "groups"

No. 53

Scales in octaves in the 24 keys

Before starting on the scales, it might be useful to revive some exercises from No. 32 and No. 34 f. The actual preparatory exercises for the scales in octaves are: thumb and fifth finger alone, legato and staccato: For the legato, aim for almost a glissando movement gliding horizontally only. Pay attention to the forward curves towards the black keys.

C major

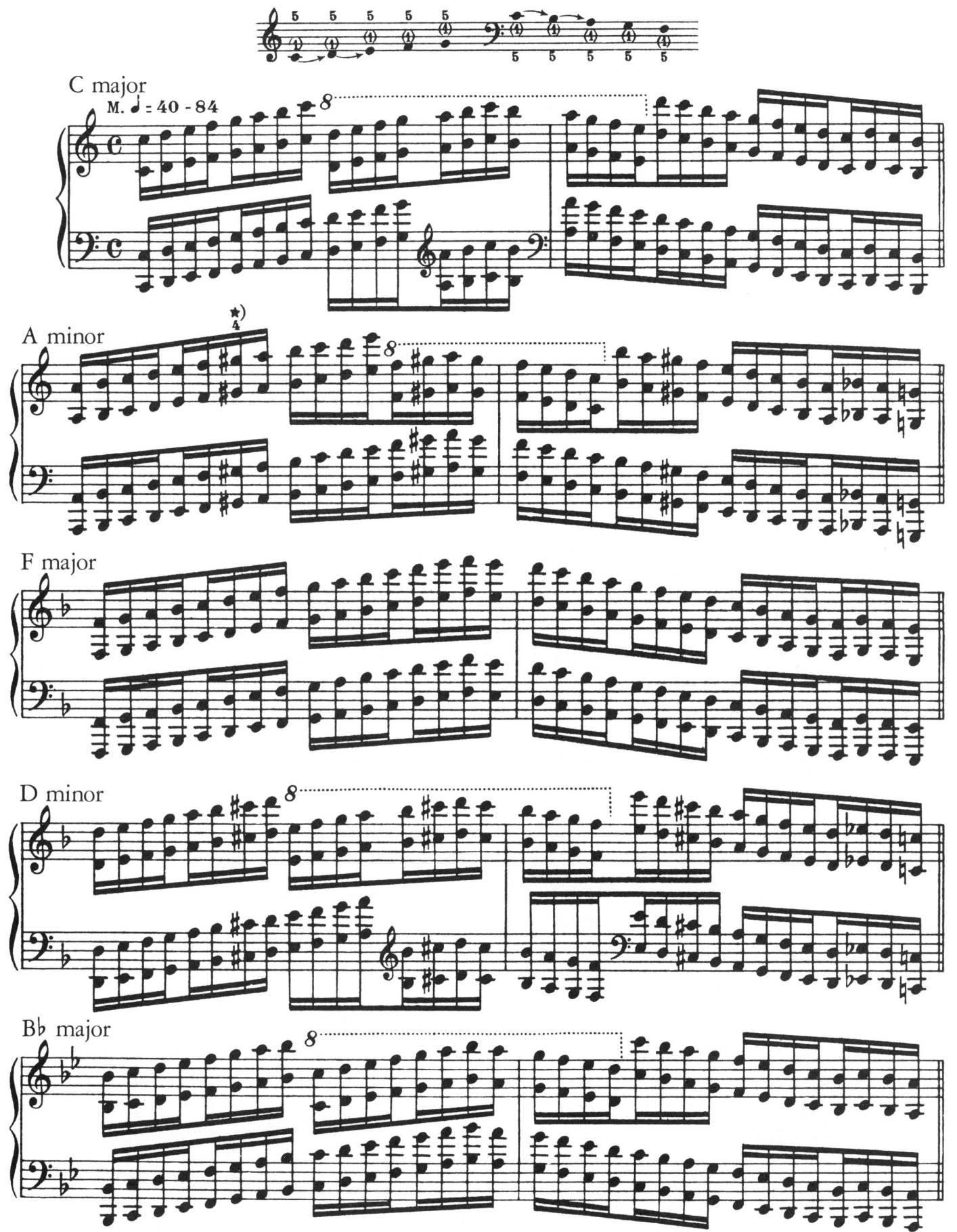

A minor

F major

D minor

B♭ major

*) In all octave progressions use the fourth finger on the black keys but only if they follow *after* a white key. For three black keys in succession use 4,5,4 or 3,4,5.

88

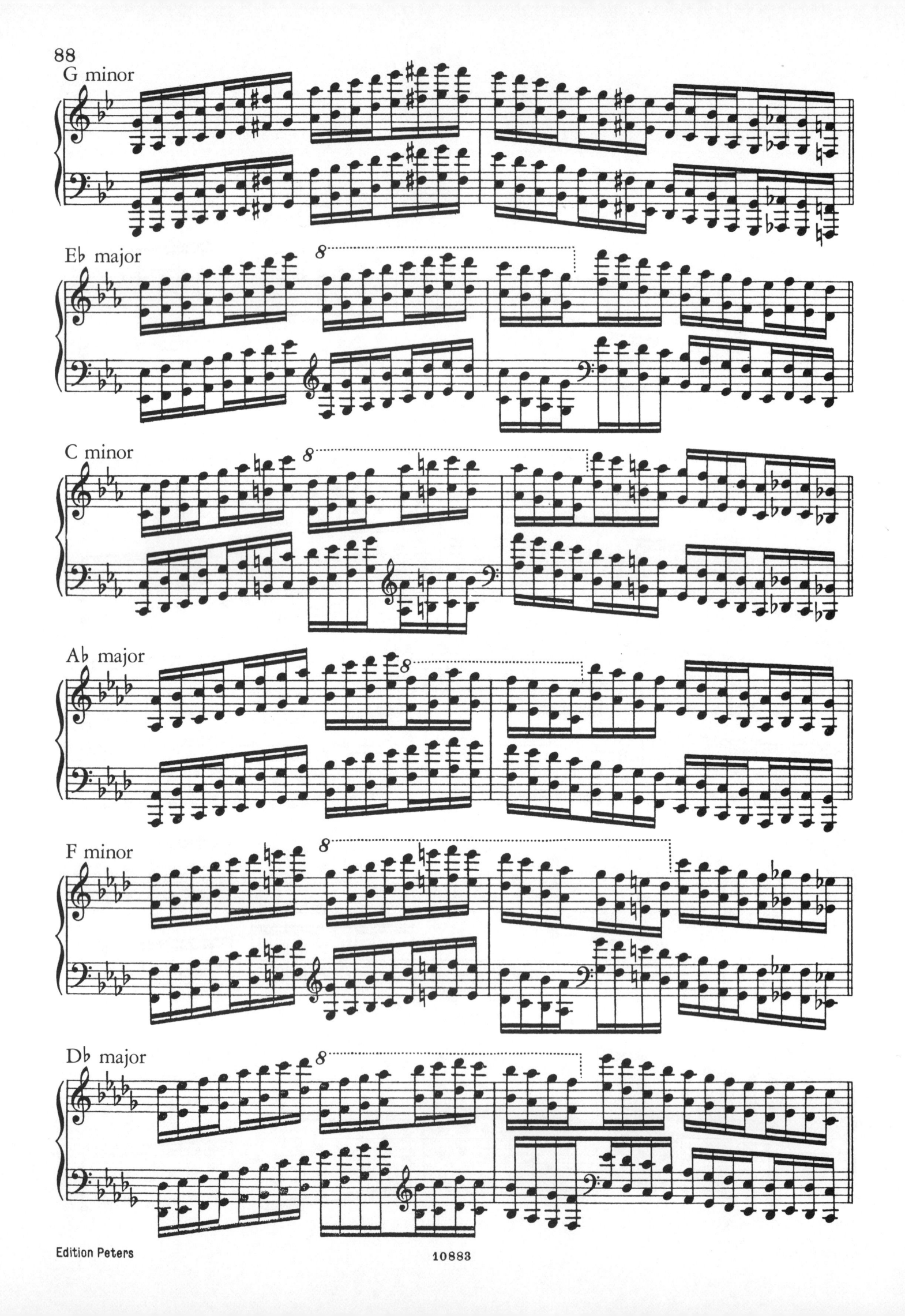

G minor

E♭ major

C minor

A♭ major

F minor

D♭ major

Bb minor

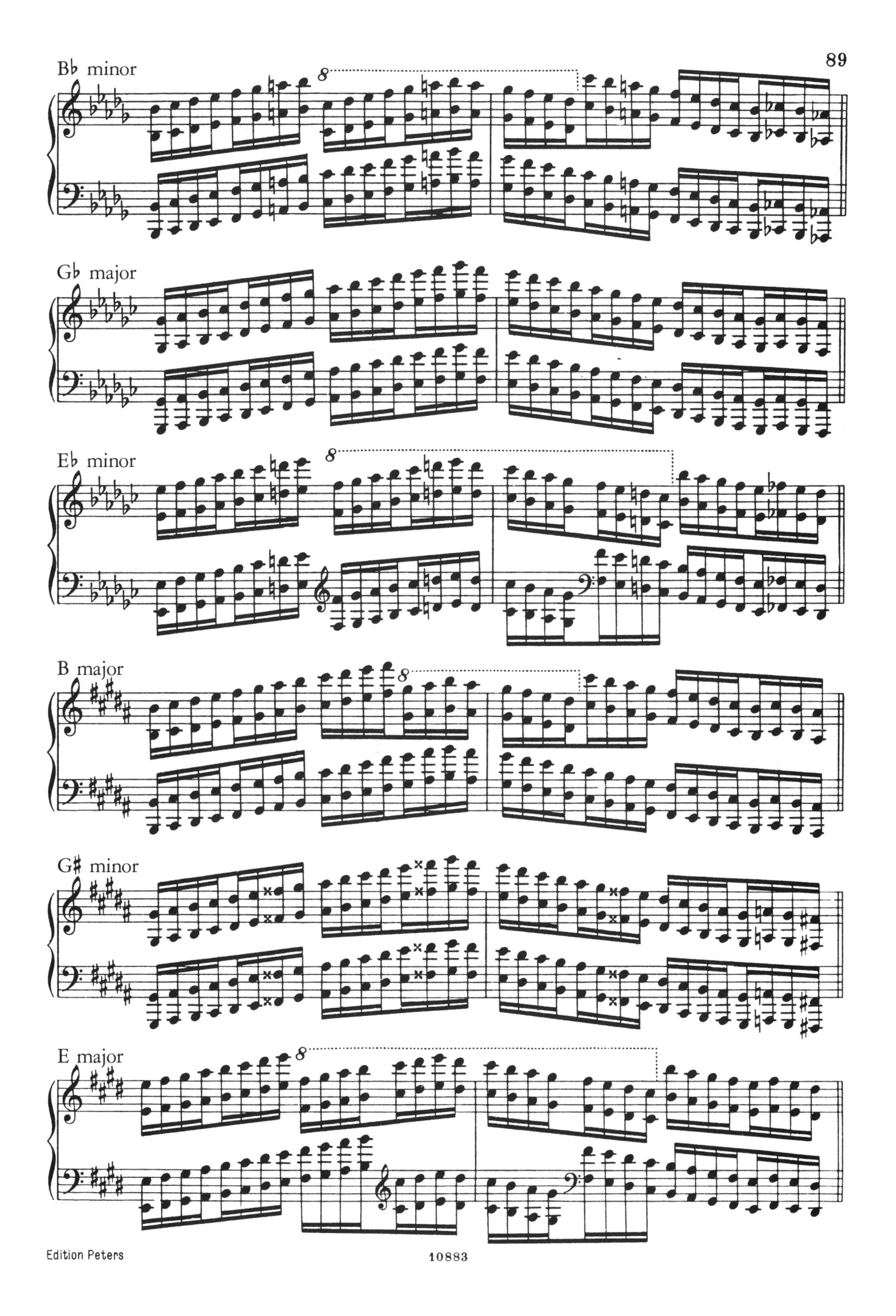

Gb major

Eb minor

B major

G# minor

E major

90

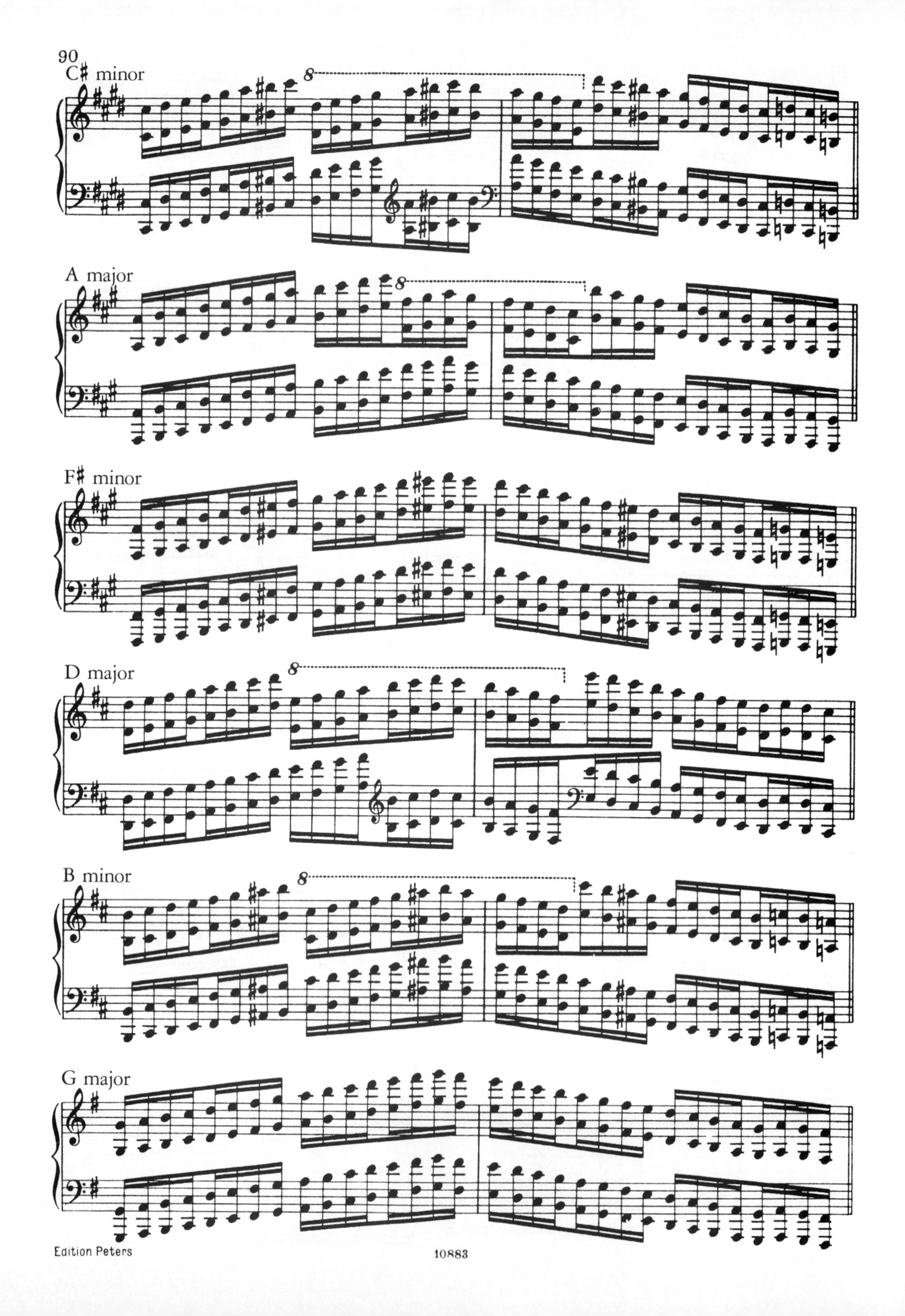

E minor

Broken

Two octaves apart

Hands separately and together

or in octaves

or in octaves

For the whole tone scale given below, play each hand separately first and note the succession of chords.

Both hands alternating

whole tone

Proceed chromatically

No. 54

Double trill in thirds for all five fingers

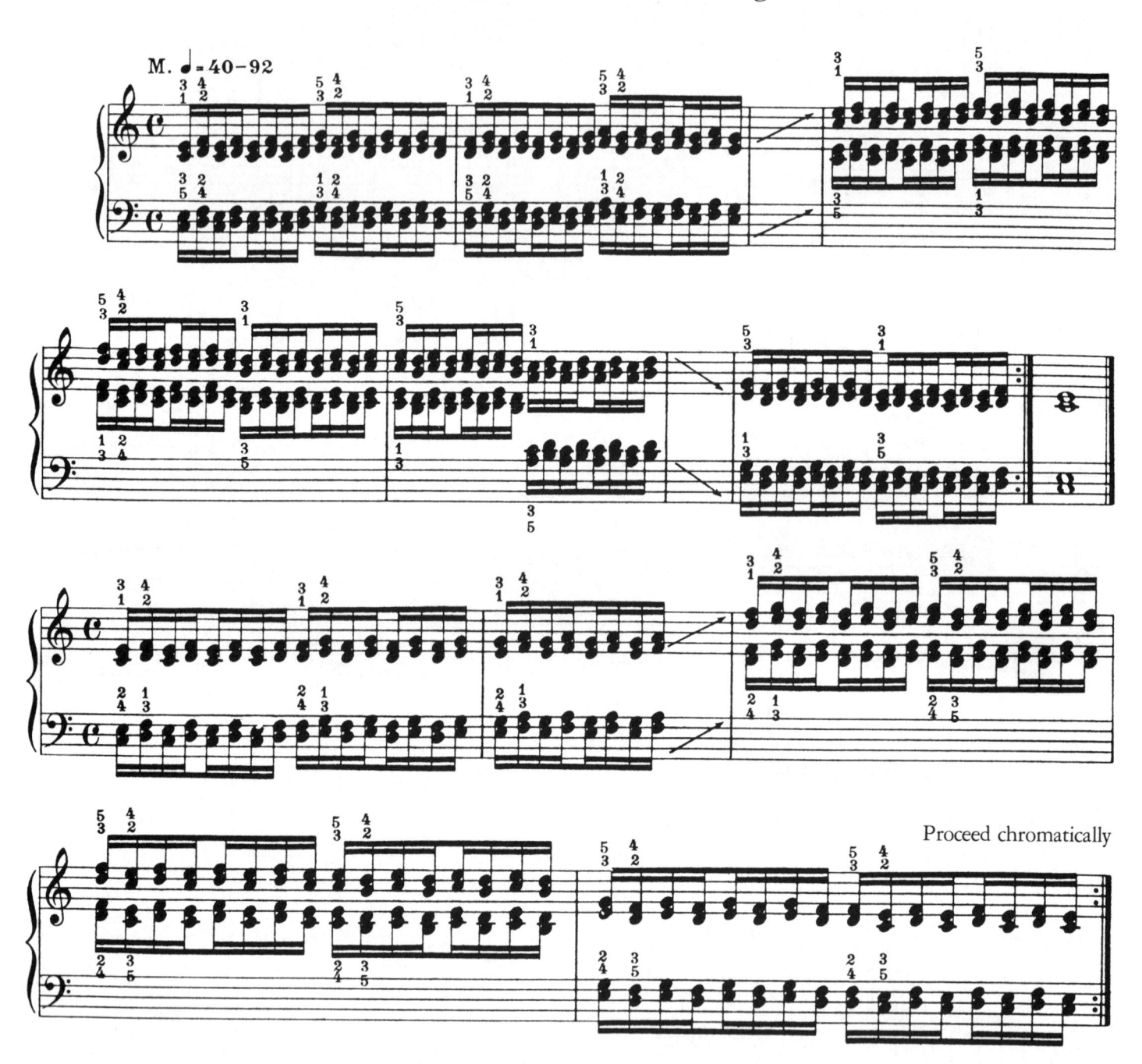

Proceed chromatically

No. 55

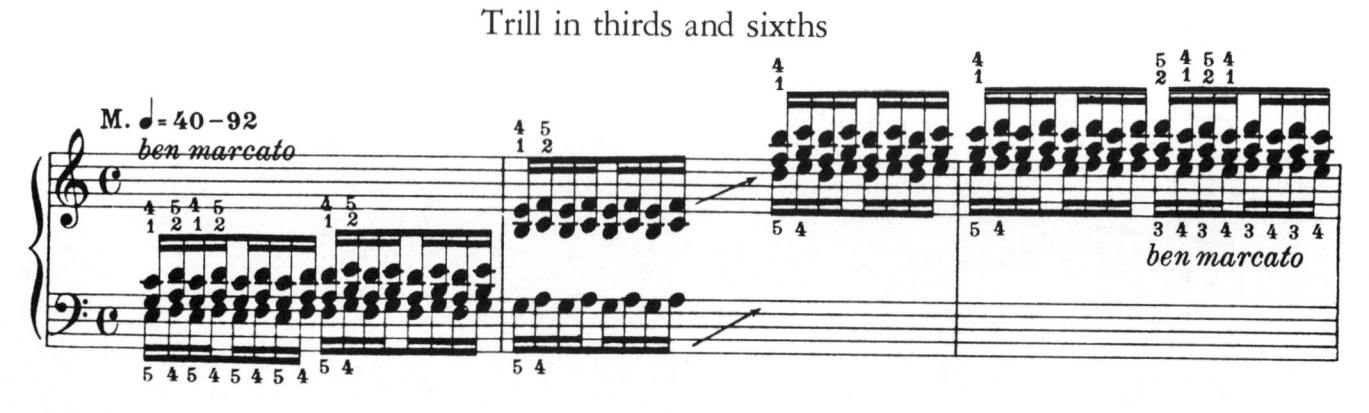

Trill in thirds and sixths

The latter is often easier in practice!

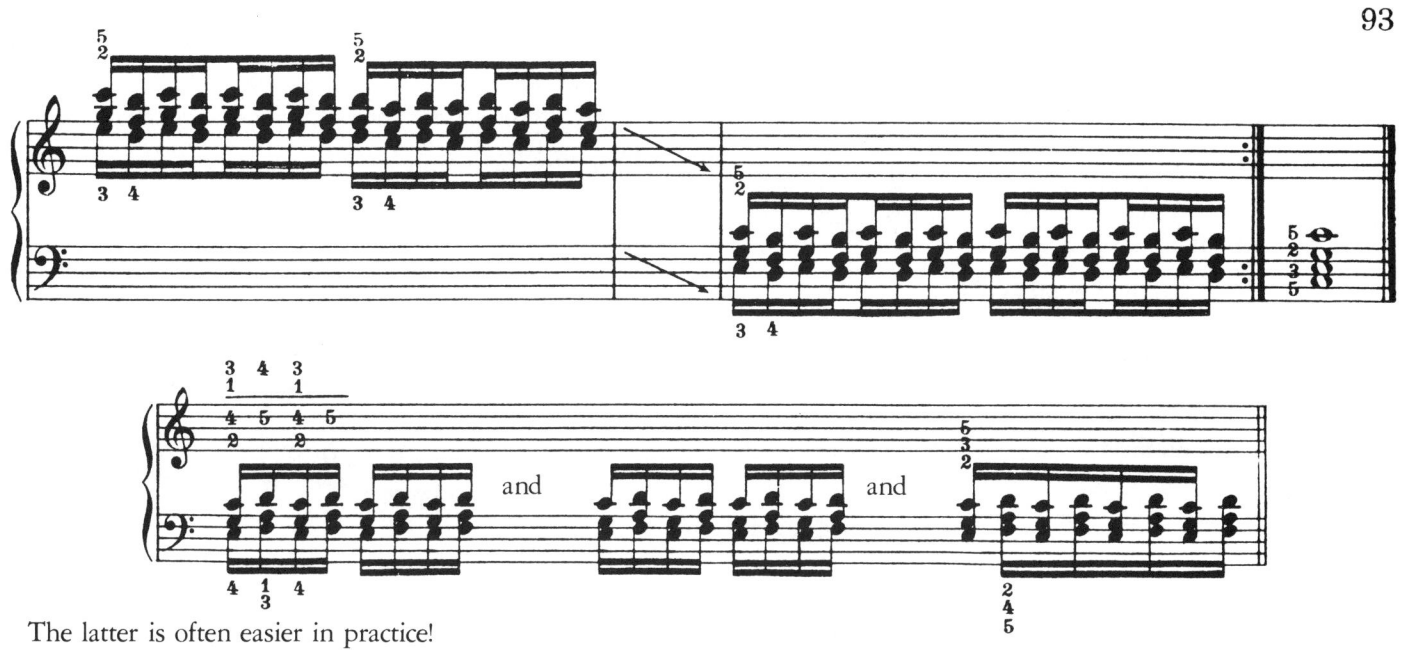

Special fingering for the fourfold trill

Another fingering

No. 56
Scales in broken octaves

Perform without interruption. Practise also as a tremolo repeating every octave several times.

C major
M. ♩=60-120

A minor

go on as in No. 53

tenths

*) In all these exercises the black keys have to be played with the 4th finger of each hand

Many exercises from the first two chapters are suitable for broken octaves: e.g. No. 2 (15), 10 (6), 11 (2), 16 (2,3), 17 (2) et al.

No. 57
Broken chords in octaves in all keys

The black keys with the 4th and 5th fingers of each hand as preferred.

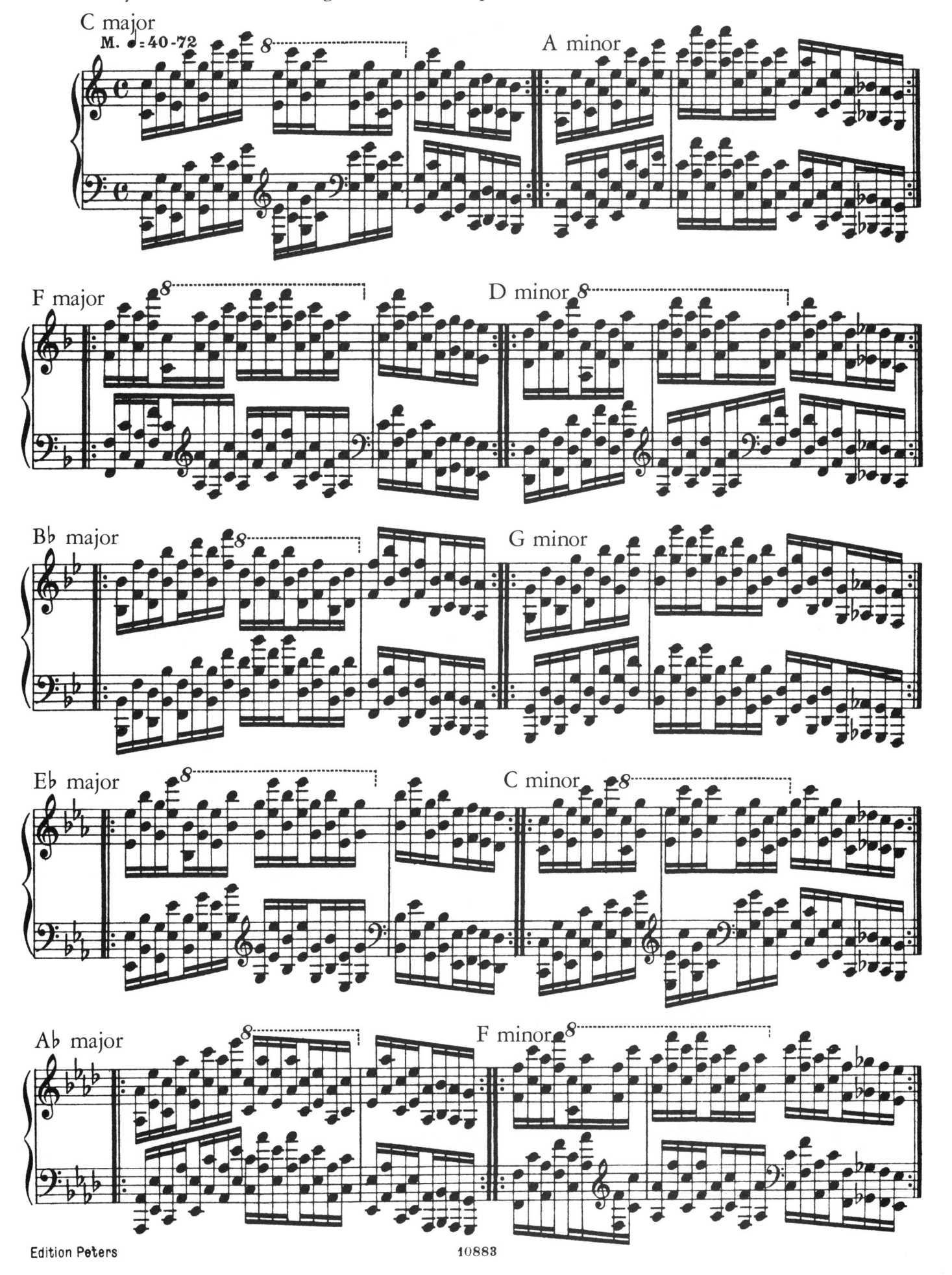

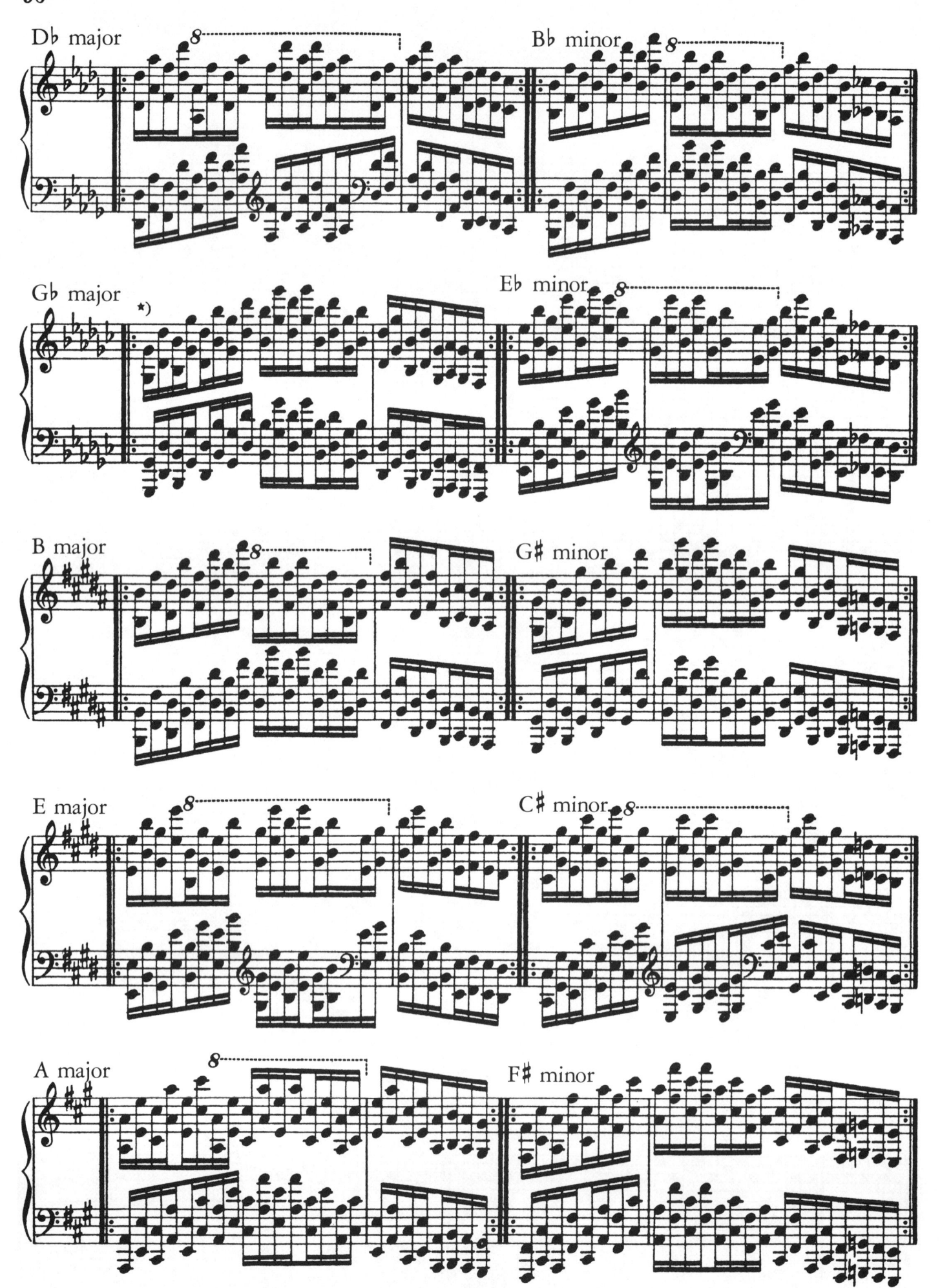

*) As this and the E♭ minor arpeggio are played on black keys only, it doesn't matter whether they start with the 4th or 5th finger. Everybody must find the fingering they prefer.

D major
B minor
G major
E minor
Also with this rhythm
Slowly, good legato
Left and right
anticipating alternately
And back

98 Broken octaves

No. 58
Chord studies

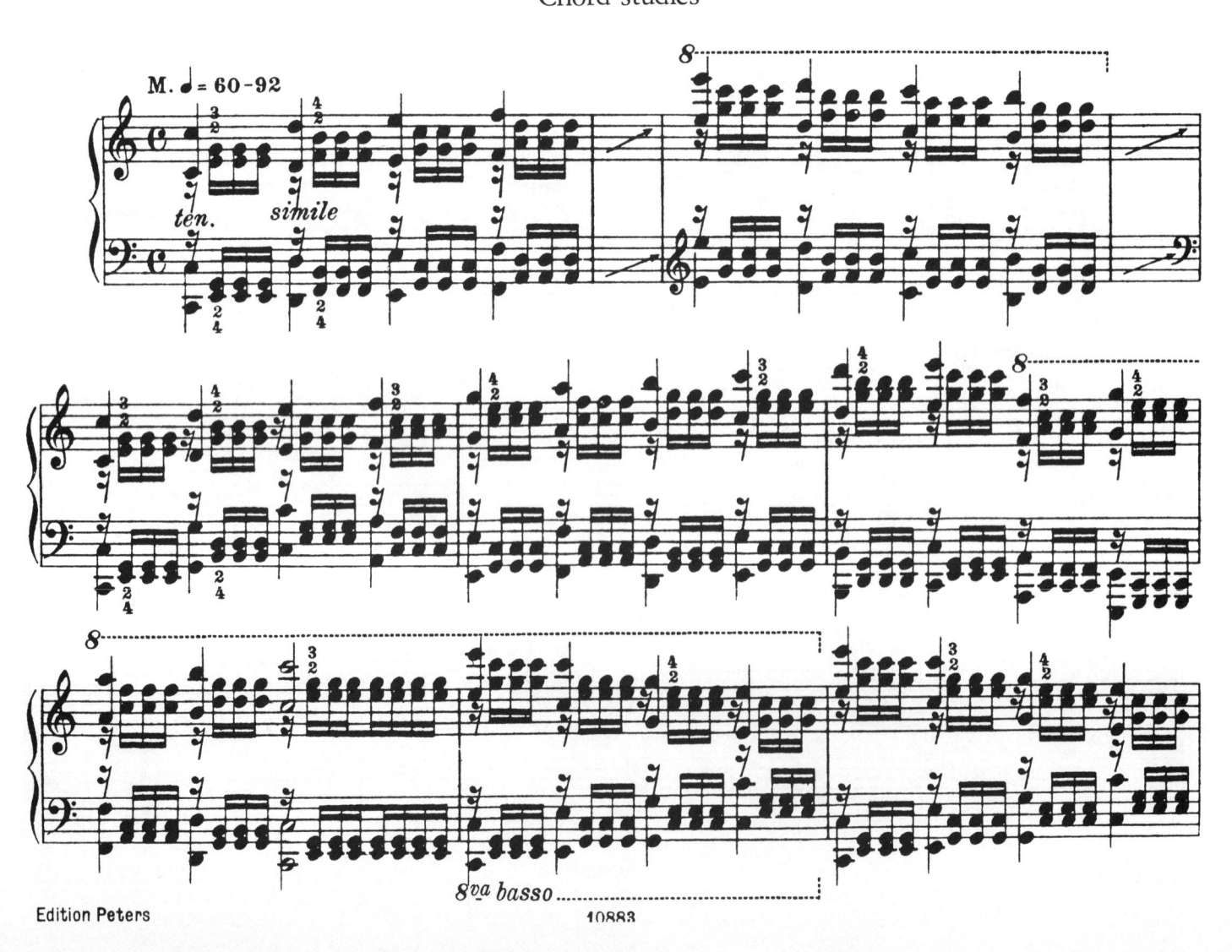

No. 59
Double trill in sixths

For stretching the 1st and 4th and the 2nd and 5th fingers of each hand.

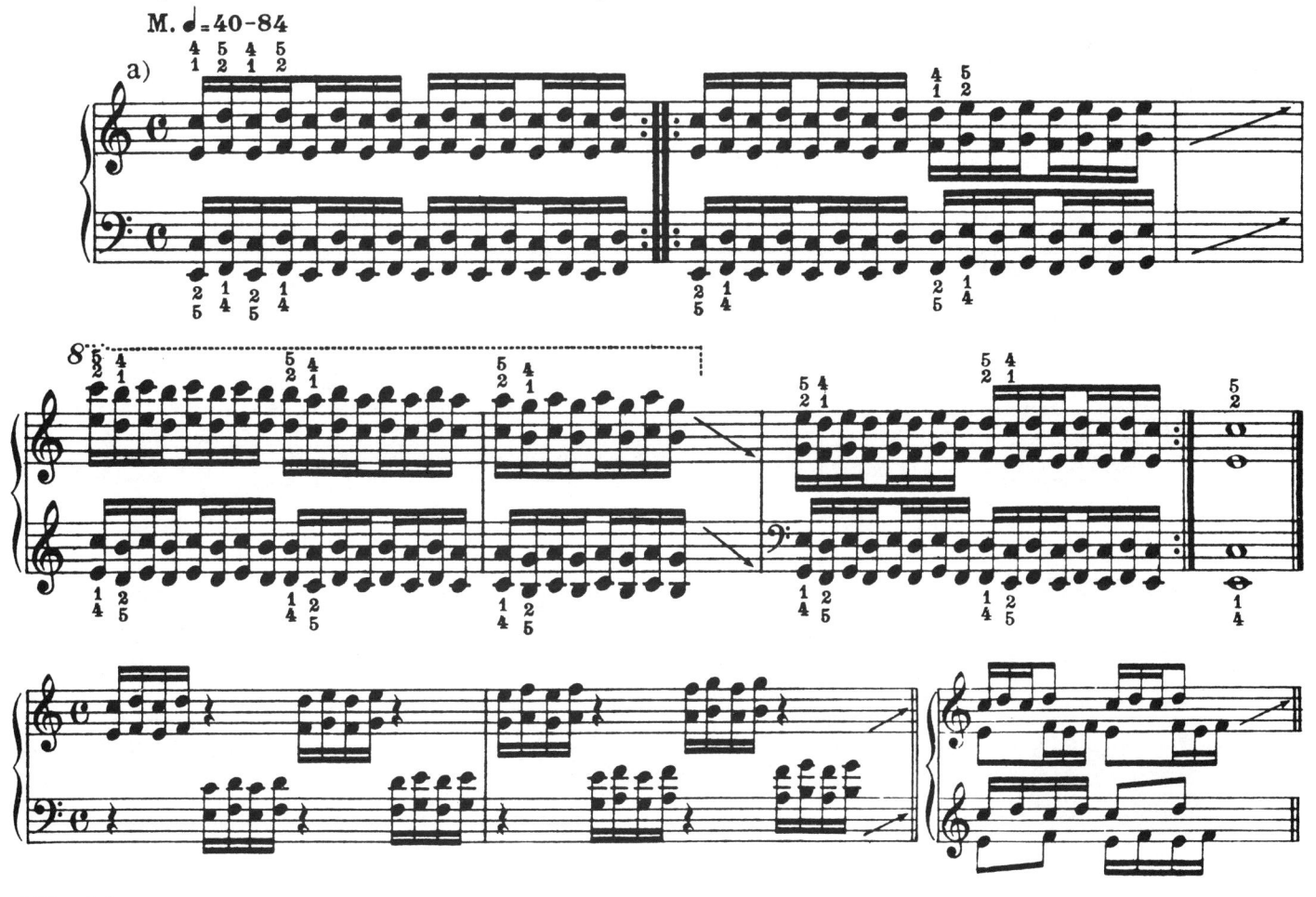

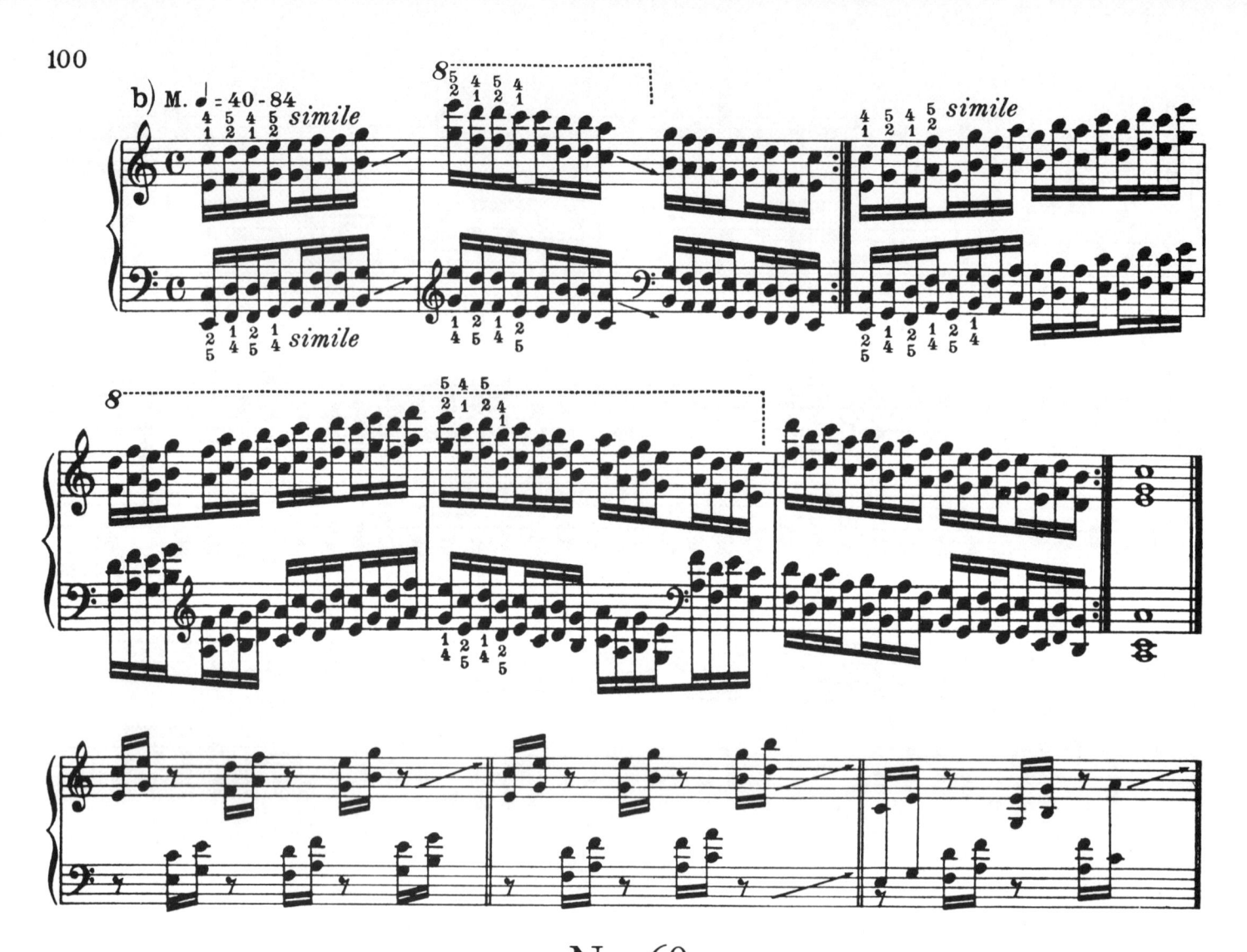

No. 60
The tremolo

To be performed effectively the tremolo must be played as quickly as a drum roll. Practise first slowly and increase the speed gradually to 72. Then increase the speed even more, letting the wrist oscillate until you reach the speed of a drum roll. This exercise is time-consuming and difficult, but the importance of the result when attained will make up for the pianist's effort to reach this goal. When Steibelt made use of his tremolo it went through his audience like a shudder. (Hanon)

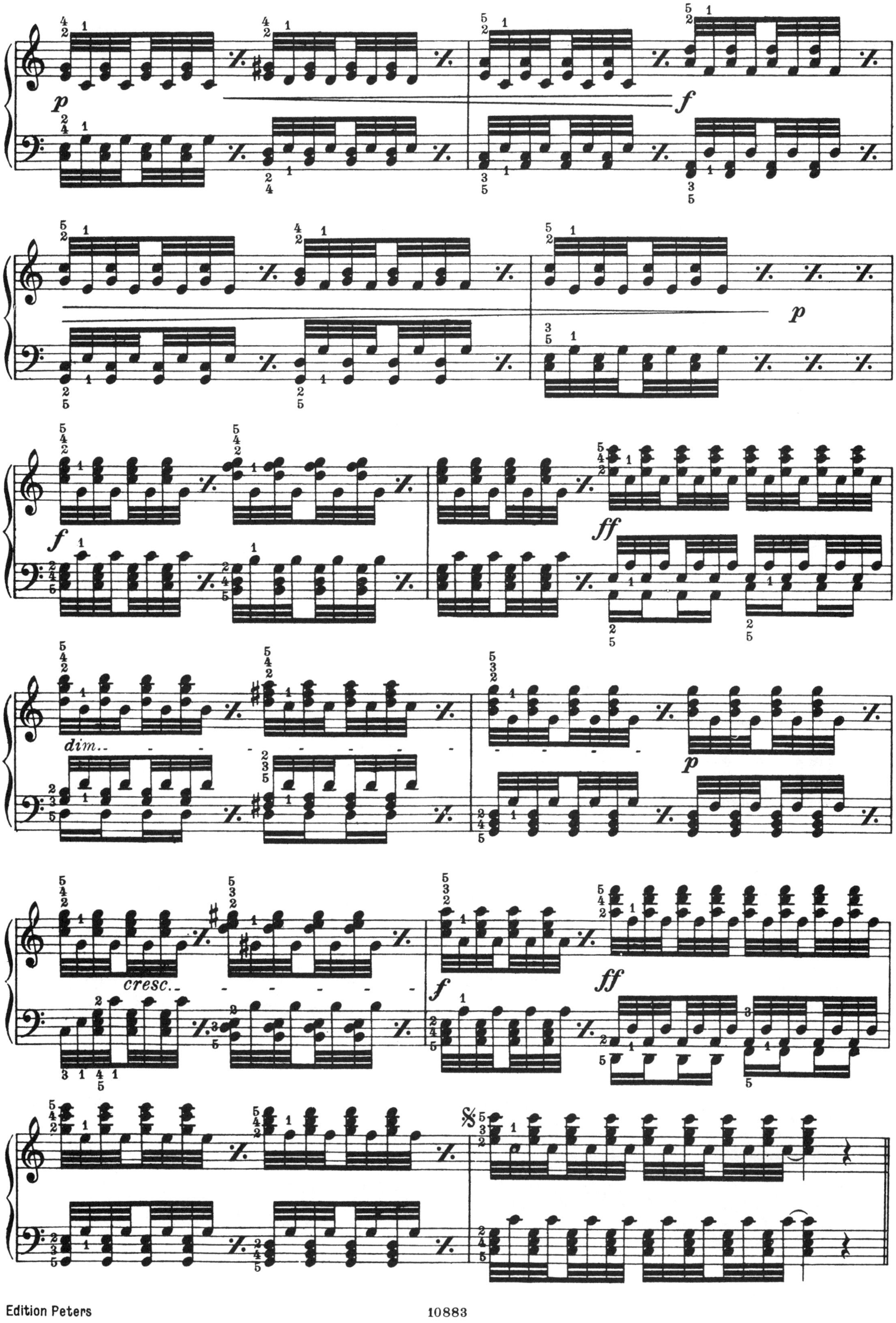
p
f
p
f
ff
dim.
p
cresc.
f
ff

102

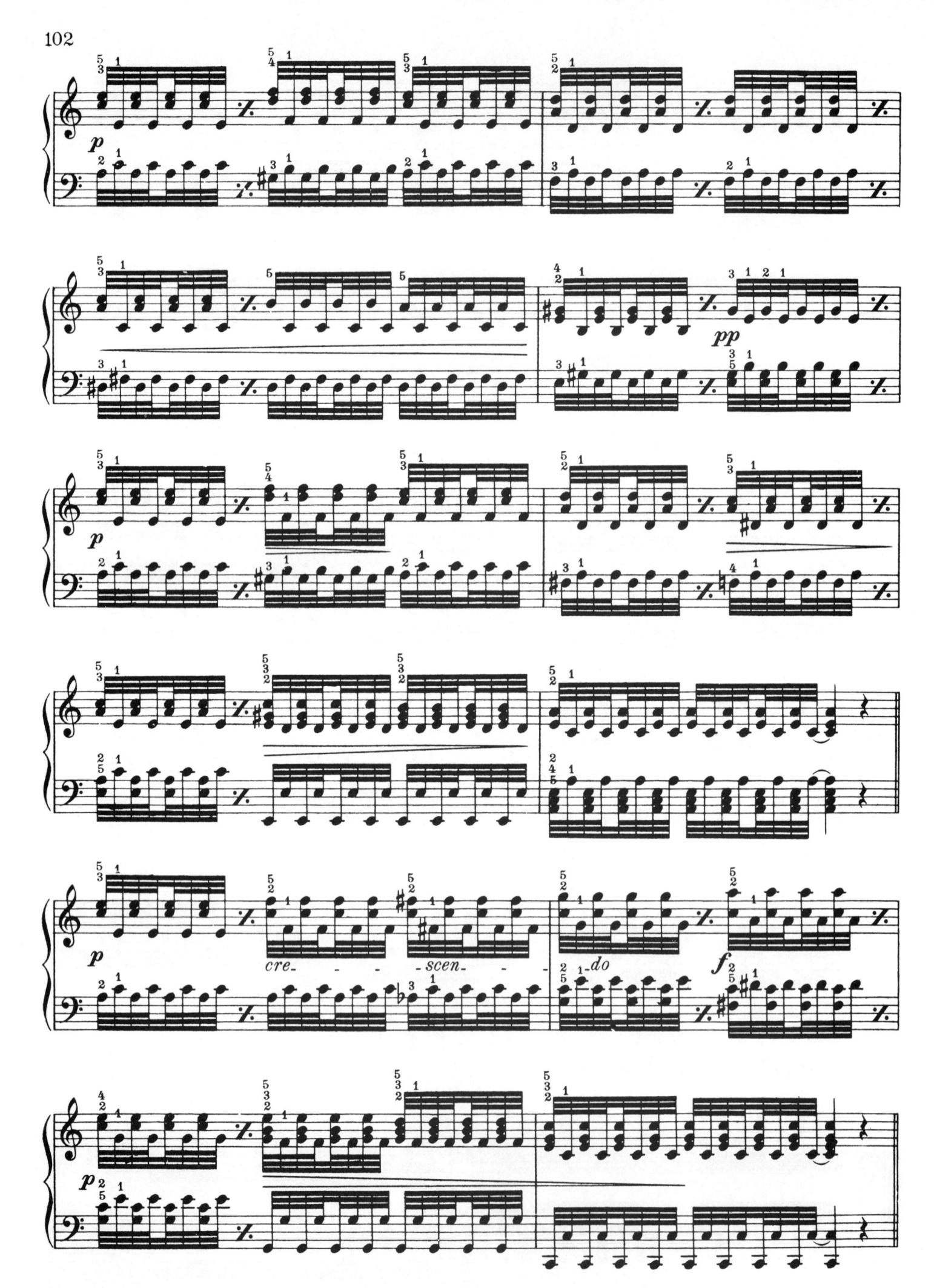

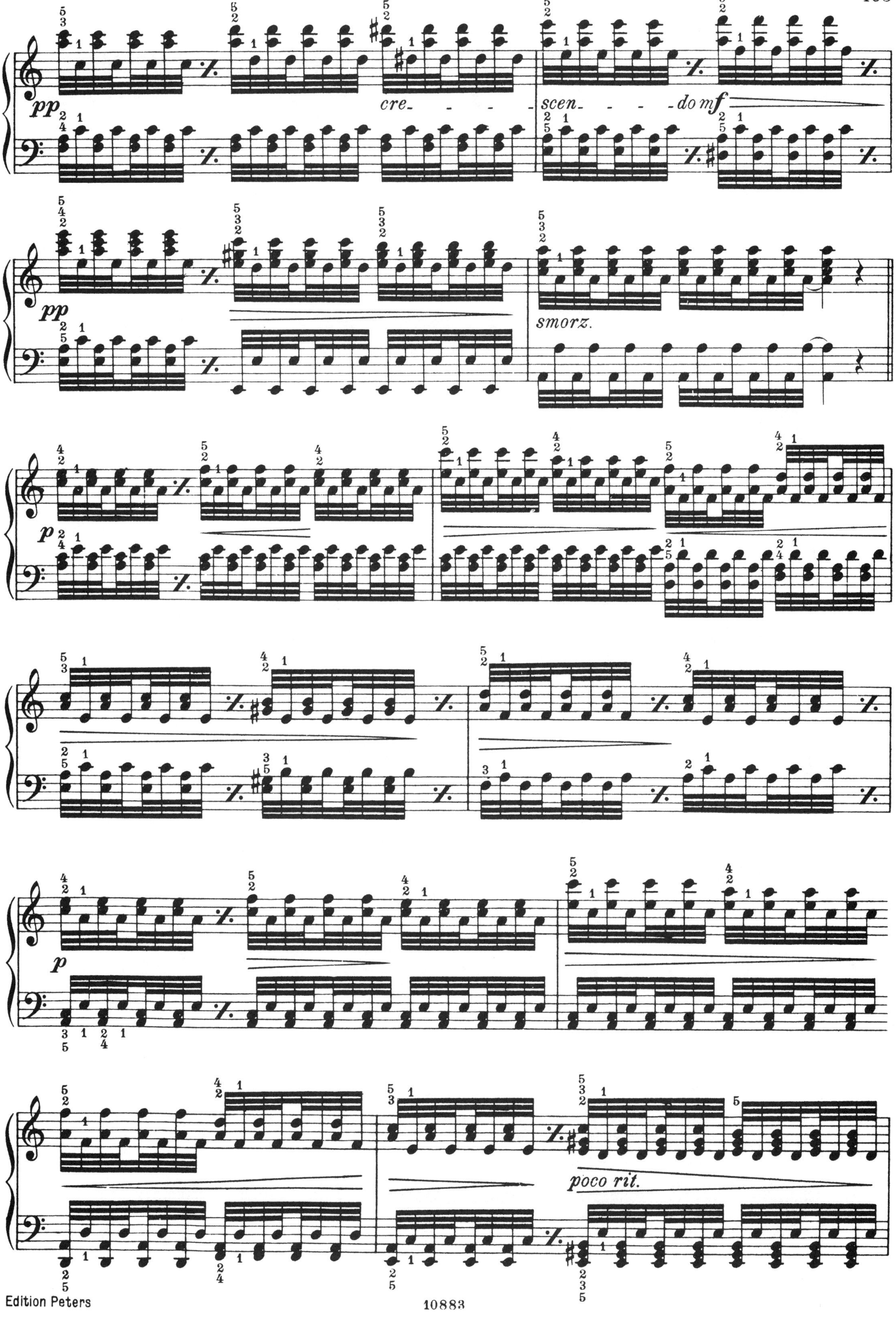
pp
cre-
scen-
do mf
pp
smorz.
p
p
poco rit.

104

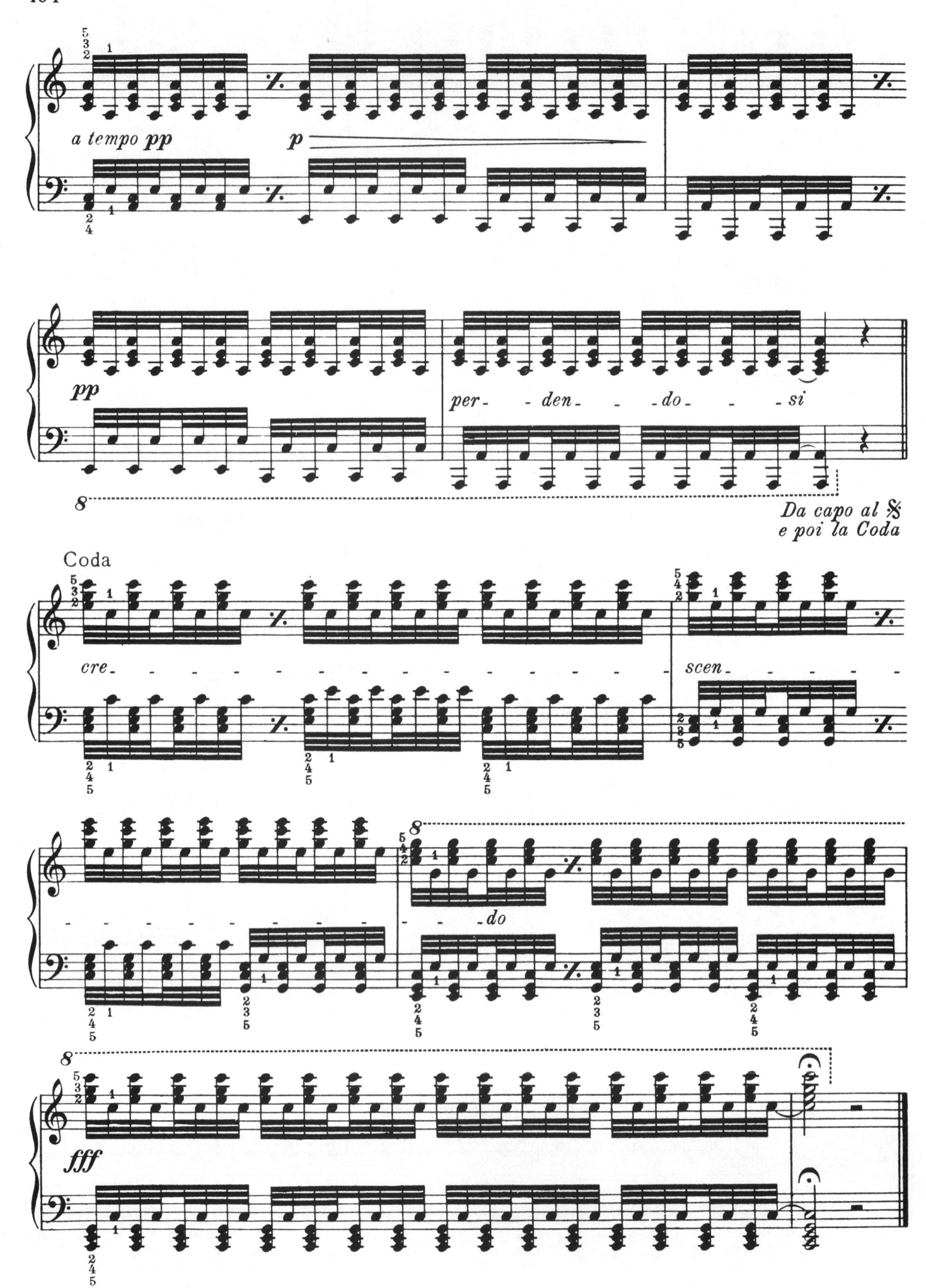